ART OF THE WORLD

NON-EUROPEAN CULTURES

THE HISTORICAL, SOCIOLOGICAL

AND RELIGIOUS BACKGROUNDS

THE ART OF
TERRACOTTA POTTERY
IN PRE-COLUMBIAN CENTRAL
AND SOUTH AMERICA

BY

ALEXANDER VON WUTHENAU

CROWN PUBLISHERS, INC., NEW YORK

Translated by the author and Irene Nicholson

Title-page: Scene from Tlatilco, as arranged in the Museo Diego Rivera, Anahuacalli, Mexico City. About 800 B.C. Approximately actual size.

Back board of jacket: left: Primitive clay sculpture with the body slit open in front. Upper Balsas River area, Guerrero. Archaic. Height 38 cm. Private collection. *Right:* Female torso. Tlatilco, plateau of Mexico. Middle pre-Classic. Height 8.2 cm. Private collection. *Cf. p. 80.*

FIRST PUBLISHED IN 1965
GERMAN EDITION © 1965 HOLLE VERLAG G.M.B.H., BADEN-BADEN, GERMANY
ENGLISH TRANSLATION © 1969 BY HOLLE VERLAG G.M.B.H.
LIBRARY OF CONGRESS CATALOG CARD NUMBER: 75-103627
PRINTED IN HOLLAND

CONTENTS

5

C. FIGURATIVE REPRESENTATIONS IN THE VARIOUS REGIONS OF MEXICO

6

LIST OF PLATES

The photographs from which the colour and black-and-white plates were taken are by the author.

The figures and map were drawn by Heinz Prüstel, Mainz, on the basis of data provided by the author.

LIST OF FIGURES

9

INTRODUCTION

Grip fast the fullest life of man, I say!
Everyone lives, each knows life little at best,
And, where you seize it, all you interest.

Goethe, Faust, *Prelude, trans. J. Todhunter*

In ancient American cultures human representations in terracotta were undoubtedly made by the million, even if we consider only those produced in the central part of the American continent. In my own hands I have held many hundred thousand clay heads which come exclusively from the region of Mexico. Over 60,000 pieces were catalogued in the private collection of the famous Mexican muralist, Diego Rivera, (which I helped to classify), the majority of them human representations. If we could not only double but increase by a hundredfold the excavations undertaken by archaeologists, the earth would probably yield a countless number of such terracotta images.

Naturally, the greater part of these objects must be considered as belonging to mass production. This holds true even for individually shaped figurines as well as for the mould-pressed pieces which were frequently made in the later epochs. But, as often happens in human life, we also come across a limited – and sometimes not so very limited – number of works which were created by true artists. The more artistic these pieces are, the more significance they have, and the more explicit is their language. They create a deeply moving impression by means of a simple synthesis and the silent impact of factual observation. One of the most startling things they reveal is an awareness and even an intimate acquaintance on the artist's part with the main characteristics of *all the races of mankind*. Archaeologically and historically it is of the utmost significance that these characteristics appeared at very early times in the art of the New World.

At this point not only the archaeologist, but precisely also the art historian should be increasingly called upon to take a hand in the work of investigation, for two main reasons: 1) to arrange the data according to geographical and chronological criteria (in so far as this is possible, considering the frequent absence of archaeological data), and 2) to classify the material according to the various styles represented (tracing their evolution from the early primitive and Archaic periods to those of maturity and late stylistic flowering, and finally to those of degeneration and decay). The overlappings, mixtures and above all the bewildering chronological and stylistic confusion which can be observed at so many early American sites should be studied and explained – or, if they cannot be explained, at least indicated.

In studying the history of art it is almost always useful and advisable to compare objects – in this case human representations – and thus in this study comparisons will be made with significant and relevant pieces found over the vast expanse of the American continent and also beyond the western hemisphere. In this way similarities and dissimilarities in technique and appearance and their significance will be established and made clear.

All this is by no means an unimportant activity, considering the present-day expansion of the concepts of art and art history. A further consideration is that ancient American art touches upon themes which will be of increasing interest to large numbers of people at various cultural levels and which will, above all, afford archaeologists and ethnologists indications and reference points for future research. Particularly in these fields it is important to overcome the 'disease of our time', exaggerated specialization, with its menace of atrophying the integral man. Our aims should be raised higher, wider, and be all-embracing. Sooner or later we will also have to get away from the one-sided, European way of looking at things. Future developments will teach us more and more to consider questions of art on a global scale, both in the present as well as in investigations of the past, particularly the human past. What do we really know about the people of early times? In Europe, in Asia and in parts of Africa material has come to light to tell us something, but so far as the huge American continent is concerned, now inhabited by a great part of the world's population, we know miserably little.

The collection of images of almost 350 different individuals published in this book is intended to promote a better understanding of man in America. And this is quite possible, precisely because of the astounding artistic achievements of a unique people. Everything has been expressed in their simple clay sculpture! What charm emanates from these usually very small masterpieces! How eloquently and directly they speak from man to man. How impressively they reveal a variety of ideas. How great is their ability to conceive and express – with greatest simplicity – the essential. And finally, how striking is the strength and exuberantly vital composure common to all these representations, which distinguishes them markedly from similar achievements of the people of other continents.

The book of pre-Columbian art is a very thick book, of which only two-thirds are generally known, sometimes just the last pages, which present us with numerous deities that are quite difficult to understand, and a pretentious system of strange and fanatical religious beliefs, dictatorially and oppressively enforced.

The material illustrated in this present work is not concerned with any 'gods' and has nothing to do with complicated problems of a mystical or religious hue. It is only concerned with the investigation of the subterranean sources of pre-Columbian art in its strictly human manifestations, employing archaeological discoveries which chiefly stem from Mexican sites and to a great extent are found in private collections. It is the result of fifteen years of investigation, related to my lectures on the history of Mexican art at Mexico City College (now the University of the Americas).

All the photographs in the book were taken by the author, with the exception of those depicting the magnificent Guatemalan incense-burner, which were procured from the photographic files of the PLATE P. 164 Musée de l'Homme in Paris. In taking these pictures, I was careful to illuminate the objects more or less from above; the reason being that the pre-Columbian artists worked, presumably without exception, in direct sunlight. They were not accustomed to working in the diffuse north light found in the studios of present-day artists. Furthermore, I made an effort to get the correct angle in the photograph to approximate the viewpoint of the artist when he modelled

13

the objects. I was also careful to avoid the centralized, rectangular views so often found in museum reproductions. My special concern was to catch the essential facial expression and the natural sculptural forms of the bodies so as to display the artistic intent and creative abilities of the ancient American artists.

To all my friends, connoisseurs and collectors, inside and outside Mexico, among whom I would like to mention especially Josué Saenz, Franz Feuchtwanger, Kurt Stavenhagen, Dr. Milton Leof, and Antonio Creixell, who had to endure repeatedly my molesting efforts at photography, I wish to express my deep gratitude. The same holds true for my friend Carlos Pellicer, who made it possible for me to take the picture in the Diego Rivera Museum (Anahua-calli) which adorns the title-page of this book, and to Dr. Eisleb, who took such good care of me in the Museum of Berlin-Dahlem, and to the Directors of the Völkerkundemuseen in Hamburg and Vienna.

If this book, as a first attempt, helps to dispel prejudices, to furnish new and unknown material for scientific research, and to stimulate and satisfy an ever-increasing group of readers who are eager for recently acquired knowledge, its purpose will have been accomplished.

San Angel, Mexico August 1965   Alexander von Wuthenau

A. THE PRINCIPAL PROBLEMS

I. CHRONOLOGY

In America the use of fired clay (termed ceramics) did not occur in any form before the middle of the third millennium BC. This assumption coincides more or less with recent reports of excavations made by Clifford Evans in Esmeraldas, Ecuador and by Ellen and Charles Brush on the Pacific coast of Mexico, south of Acapulco at Puerto Marquez. Thus, for instance, a radio-carbon dating of 4400 (± 140) was calculated from the lowest level, No. 33, at Puerto Marquez (eleven metres down) which gives a date corresponding roughly to the year 2500 BC.

Earliest ceramic finds

It may be that these excavations were made in especially deep and therefore early layers. In any case, in view of the latest findings in archaeological research, surprises are the order of the day. In many parts of the American continent recent excavations have yielded dates indicating earlier habitation than has previously been supposed, and probably the trend toward earlier dating will continue. Generally speaking, however, the manufacture of ceramics (particularly of human images, our main concern in this book) may not have occurred much before 2000 BC. About the year 1500 BC products of the early pre-Classic epoch (*preclásico inferior*) appeared at a variety of sites in the Americas. In most archaeological studies the following dates have come to be accepted for subdivisions of the first epoch of pre-Columbian art in Mexico (the pre-Classic or Archaic period):

1) early pre-Classic   1660 – 1000 BC
2) middle pre-Classic   1000 – 600 BC
3) late pre-Classic   600 BC – 300 AD

Threefold classification

More exact dating for this almost unknown but extremely interesting period will require a great deal of anthropological research. An internationally organized group of scholars to gather data and solve the problems of dating, etc. would be highly desirable. Because of the enormous number of archaeological sites in the New World

(Mexico alone has about 12,000), an intensive exploration cannot possibly be handled by persons from one country. A promising sign of future co-operation is the fact that in 1965 Germany sent scholars to participate in excavations and studies of sites from the earliest epochs in the state of Puebla. The obstacles to be overcome are many: for vast areas have never been explored, let alone charted for scientific digging. This is particularly true of the western provinces and Guerrero. Nevertheless, a start toward international co-operation has been made. For our investigation of the history of art in pre-Columbian America the simple tripartite division of the pre-Classic era given above will suffice.

Classic era The period after the beginning of the Christian era, considerably better known, is usually subdivided as follows:

  1) early Classic   300 – 600 AD
  2) late Classic   600 – 900 AD.

This epoch is also called the 'theocratic period' or the 'Golden Age of Mexico'. While the pre-Classic period is distinguished by an enormous variety of clay sculpture and the beginnings of stonework, the Classic period presents us with an intensive development in architecture, namely the erection of grandiose religious centres, aesthetically very well planned, and a more mature production in the fields of sculpture and painting.

Post-Classic era The Classic epoch was succeeded by the post-Classic, subdivided as follows:

  1) early post-Classic   900 AD – 1300 AD
  2) late post-Classic   1300 AD – 1521 AD.

This period is also called the 'early historic' and the 'historic' because of the availability of genuine historical sources for its study, such as the native Indian records called codices (pictorial writings,

The two heads *(a)* and *(b)*, among the most primitive products of pre-Columbian art, are from the early pre-Classic period, Guerrero. All figures of this kind have bodies that are slit open in front (cf. reverse of slip-case and text, p. 80). *(c)*, *(f)*: two interesting pieces from Veracruz. *(d)*, *(e)*: two small heads from the coastal area of Guerrero; *(d)* is from the late pre-Classic and *(e)* from the middle pre-Classic. Height: *(a)* 15 cm, *(b)* 18 cm, *(c)* 15 cm, *(d)* 4.3 cm, *(e)* 3.9 cm, *(f)* 12.5 cm. *Cf. pp. 23, 131.*

b

d

e

f

glyphs, etc. from both before and after the Spanish conquest). Many writings on historical matters by Europeans are also available.

During the post-Classic era architectural activity continued on a grand scale, although restricted more or less to the traditional styles of preceding times. In the other arts, however, an acute stylization developed, and even what can be called the over-stylization of a late epoch. Toward the end of the period everything became submerged in the complicated, 'divine' world of the Aztecs, the last group to appear on the pre-Columbian scene. They also achieved, however, a sublime artistic expression in their stone sculpture, which immediately impresses us with its strength and truly monumental style.

In the field of ceramics, the first place for excellent work must be given to the post-Classic Mixtecs of Oaxaca, who wrote the last chapter on American soil in ceramic work with a delicate and sensitive hand. They can also be considered as probably the most talented writers of codices. Since this last activity continued beyond the conquest, we are able to see not only the Indians as they were depicted by the Spaniards, but also the Europeans as they were depicted by the Indians. A few pictures and notes on this particular cultural achievement will be included at the end of the book, to give due credit to this last flowering of ancient art on the American continent.

Mould-cast figures. The expressive heads *(a)* and *(b)* originate from the Huasteca area. This technique apparently must have been used there as well as at Teotihuacán during the pre-Classic period. *(d)*: typical mould-cast figurine of the Toltec Mayapán style (post-Classic), found at Veracruz. By virtue of the precise modelling, it differs greatly from the realistic heads *(a)* and *(b)*. The development of this ever-increasing stylization in Toltec ceramic figurines apparently originates with early products in Guerrero. This can be shown with a fair degree of certainty on the basis of terracotta finds (cf. pp. 84, 104). *(c)*: late mould-cast figure, stylistically derived from Teotihuacán, the features clearly those of an idol. *Cf. p. 23.*

II. THE TECHNIQUES

'Burnt clay, apart from being breakable, is practically indestructible.' This simple definition, taken from the amusing and witty book of Peter Bamm, *On the Shores of Light*, states with matchless brevity a great deal about the essence of ceramics. It explains the boundless ocean of broken sherds, in Mexico called *tepalcates*, which plays such an important part in the activities of archaeologists. How often is a small piece of burnt clay the first (and sometimes for a long period the only) testimony a scholar finds to mark the existence of an otherwise unknown culture! Peter Bamm's definition also emphasizes the surprising resistance that ceramics, especially when well-fired, put up against all destructive agents. Pieces of pottery thousands of years old have been excavated which look as though they emerged from the kiln the day before. Mexico has many examples of such objects.

To be sure, the manufacture of ceramics was subject to a variety of fluctuating influences in pre-Columbian times, yet certain characteristics are common to all the burnt clay objects produced in this epoch. In the formation of these characteristics we may consider as *Absence of* of prime importance the absence of the potter's wheel and also of *potter's wheel* other mechanical devices (at least in the early periods).

Modelling Thus all ancient American terracotta sculpture required a direct modelling of the bulk of the material, and the full creative power of the artist was called into play at every moment. This is why the pieces are so alive and so full of charm. At the first glance one immediately recognizes and unconsciously feels the directness of the artist's approach, expressed in every plane, in every detail. The technique is also conducive to the expression of a great variety of ideas, both in the making of pottery proper and in the creating of figurative representations.

Pastillage As well as the technique of block modelling, in very early times that called *pastillage* was employed. In this method use is made of small strips or coils or particles of clay, which are joined or stuck to the main body of the piece. In making pottery coils were used to build up the shape of the vessel, and in the creation of figure sculpture the coils and particles were used to enliven the forms and to achieve variety in the representation of the human face. The fantasy of the artist was given unlimited scope, and the results embraced the whole realm of expression, from the most primitive to the most sophisticated.

If we take into consideration merely the form of the human eye, we immediately see that the technique of representation was continuously subject to change and variation. For instance, the well-known 'coffee-bean' eye of the pre-Classic period, which was derived from the squeezing technique of a previous epoch, is found in oval, extremely long, slanting or round shapes. When applied so as to flow into the planes of the face it achieves a startlingly artistic and almost classical effect (as in the early vertical heads from Guerrero). The attempt has been made to place into an orderly system the great number of techniques used to render eyes. The American anthropologist, George Vaillant, has been a pioneer in this field, particularly in regard to the classification of the pre-Classic epoch in the high plateau of Mexico. Miguel Covarrubias and others developed the system further. The classification into types A, D, C, K, etc. can be helpful to archaeologists in their studies. But it will probably never be possible to arrange all the different types into a neat and all-inclusive system. The differentiation into mixed types and cross-breeds, for instance those found in combinations of *pastillage* with other techniques, makes for a cumbersome system, whose manipulation could well be a hobby for virtuosi. The existence of such an abundance of ideas and the variety of ways in which they were applied defy every attempt at classification.

The eye
PLATE P. 19

With the introduction of moulds into the production of ceramic objects, the technical complications increased, for an indefinite repetition of cast units was made possible. A great number of casting moulds have been found in Mexican archaeological excavations. In the south (Guerrero) and in the east (the area of the Huasteca), this technique must have been used in very early times and evidently

Moulds

PLATE P. 20

23

led to a very sensitive and highly artistic expression in clay. The great period of mould-cast works was that of Teotihuacán, in the central valley of Mexico (still continued in our day!). In the Classic period the well-known little 'portrait' heads of innumerable figurines were rendered individually significant by specialists trained in refined retouching techniques. The Maya also used moulds in great profusion, often combining their use with a highly developed method of *pastillage* application, with a very acceptable result. Aztec moulded ceramics, on the other hand, often degenerated into a rather uninteresting product, due to banal and consequently lifeless repetition.

Preparation of clay body The preparation of the clay body as well as the firing procedure varied a great deal from region to region and were often linked to the natural occurrence of various substances in the clay. Even in early times, surprisingly enough, the body of the clay was mixed in technically correct amounts with mineral substances (quartz crystals, crushed obsidian, mica etc.) to make a practical, durable ceramic. The employment of kaolin (porcelain earth) by Olmec master ceramists began in early times (middle pre-Classic). These artists must have had excellent firing techniques and special kilns, whereas in other regions open fires were still being used for the production of a very primitive ware.

Colouring Great importance was attached to the colour of the ceramics, which depended upon a correct choice of clay specimens, considering their native properties and the length of firing time. By painting mineral substances on the dried clay objects before firing (the application of slip), pre-Columbian potters achieved a remarkable variety of shades: light and dark, reddish brown and white; when combined these gave a special effect to the overall design of the final product. The finer ceramic articles were polished with incredible artistic skill, using fine instruments such as agate stones. The result was a hard, smooth and brilliant surface, which could resist very well the effects of time, moisture and burial in the soil, which is chemically

PLATE P. 29 disintegrating. The decoration of ceramics by painting, especially for use as burial gifts, is a chapter unto itself. This was done with whitewash or cinnabar; the pigments have often been preserved and are visible on many clay figurines.

III. THE SITES

The concept of Mesoamerica, invented by archaeologists, is relatively new. Ignacio Bernal speaks of *sur-espace* and a *supra-région culturelle*. Mesoamerica comprises the middle section of the American continent, approximately from the southern border of the United States to the northern border of Nicaragua, and thus includes all of Mexico and most of Central America. It is in this area that the main body of pre-Columbian art was produced, and by far the most important and largest region within Mesoamerica is present-day Mexico.

Only in the last twenty-five years have the quantity and great fecundity of the archaeological sites of this country been realized. The complications of its history and the truth about the beginnings of its cultures are slowly emerging from the obscurity of the past. The development appears to have taken the form of a series of cultural waves, which successively and with a continuous, gliding and overlapping rhythm found their way into the remotest corners of Mesoamerica. It is curious that even during the most ancient pre-Classic epochs the inhabited regions were spread over a very wide area. Marking the boundaries of these extensions are innumerable ceramic artifacts, which eloquently tell the story of the energetic, vivacious and travel-eager people who lived in America during early times.

The amazing thing the artifacts reveal is that the rugged terrain of this area did not to any great extent hamper the urge to expand of these early people. Neither the extreme climatic differences between regions nor the deep valleys and *barrancas* so well described by Aldous Huxley, nor the enormous mountain ranges reaching high above the timber line, nor the rivers and swamps, nor the rock-strewn seashores, deterred many groups from migrating into all regions. All through this obscure period there must have been a constant movement of people from the damp, hot coastal strips

Topography and climate

along the Atlantic and Pacific oceans into the subtropical regions and finally up into the cool mountain areas of the plateaus and back again. In very early times trade must have taken place between all these different groups, in which a considerable amount of merchandise was exchanged. The atmosphere of continuous reciprocal influences must have been kept alive all through the pre-Columbian period, as well as during the pre-Classic epoch. It is no wonder that it is extremely difficult to delineate – schematically and precisely – definite regions and cultural borders. The quantity of exceptions will for ever prove too great for proper rules to be formed.

We do have, however, sufficient information from the evidence of archaeologists, historians, collectors etc. to circumscribe approximately the regions where ceramics of relevance and artistic importance were made. The map at the end of this book attempts to indicate these different regions.

MAP P. 190

Southern district The existence of very early archaeological sites in the southern district (District I on the map) entitles us to begin here. It is the region located to the south of our central point of reference, the area of the capital city of Mexico. This region comprises the present-day states of Guerrero and Morelos. The former state borders on the Pacific Ocean and possesses an extensive coastline, named the Costa Chica south of Acapulco and the Costa Grande to the north. The whole area has a decidedly warm but pleasant climate. Running through Guerrero from one end to the other, parallel to the sea, is a high mountain range called the Sierra Madre. Its northern and southern extensions are intersected by hundreds of fissured ravines, so that Guerrero has some of the most forbidding terrain imaginable. Almost all the ancient cultures of the pre-Columbian period left their traces successively or side by side throughout this southern district of Mexico. In the opinion of many connoisseurs Guerrero is the cradle of a variety of styles which spread over large regions and in all directions. This seems a reasonable assumption, if the evidence of the greatly varied ceramic output of the region is carefully studied.

Central plateau The next large district (District II), which before the arrival of the Spaniards already possessed an art history two thousand years old, comprises the imposing plateau of central Mexico. The area was especially favoured in every respect to become one of the focal points of the pre-Columbian world. Lying at a height of about 2300 metres, the plateau has a temperate sub-tropical climate. Its soil is fertile, water was abundant, and the landscape, with a great mirror-like lake surrounded by heavily wooded mountains, was exceptionally beautiful. The snow-capped volcanoes, Ixtacihuatl and Popocatepetl, still stand as monumental guardians at the edge of this valley, which was first settled many centuries ago by a highly gifted people. Their artistic production began with exquisite ceramics in the epoch of the pre-Classic, reached its zenith in the execution of the Teotihuacán masterpieces and continued thereafter in a more or less traditional manner until the invasion of the Spanish conquerors. The sequence came to a violent end in 1521, when the colonial period began.

Directly to the east and south-east of the plateau of Mexico are the plain of Puebla and the valley of Oaxaca (District III), both belonging to the temperate zone. The Puebla region was a counterpart to the central plateau, to the east of the famous volcanoes. *Puebla and Oaxaca*

It extended to within view of another great volcano, Pico de Orizaba, situated on the other side of the plain. The sanctuary of Cholula, with connections by road to Veracruz on the east coast and the gateways to Guerrero on the west, make the Puebla region an interesting and fertile area for archaeological investigations. Oaxaca boasts one of the most important of the pre-Columbian sacred cities, Monte Albán. This site was occupied continuously for a very long time by a tribe called the Zapotecs and later by the Mixtecs. It is considered one of the most important indigenous cultural centres of Mesoamerica.

The next or eastern zone (District IV), which extends all the way from the plateau to the Atlantic Ocean, is far more complicated than the preceding one. It lies like an enormous crescent around the Gulf of Mexico. The hinterland of this area is mountainous and subtropical, the lowlands hot and tropical with rich soil and more rainfall than anywhere else in the country. This extensive area *Eastern zone*

27

served as the stage for the development of some of the finest cultural works in Mexico.

In the north the main culture was that of the Huasteca, found on the shores of the Panuco River, which flows into the Atlantic near Tampico; in the centre is the present-day state of Veracruz, where in the midst of luxurious vegetation the talented Remojadas and Totonac artists had their abode; and finally to the south are the swamp lands and virgin forests of Tabasco, where there flourished the most mysterious of all pre-Columbian cultures, the Olmec.

Western zone The western part of Mexico (District V), which again borders on the Pacific Ocean, extends over a huge territory, from Sinaloa in the north to Michoacán in the south. On the whole it has a mild, agreeable, mostly subtropical climate. Compared with other parts of Mexico its landscapes are mellower and not so alien, and the character of its people seems to resemble that of the land. This western zone, which includes the states of Nayarit, Colima, Jalisco, and part of Guanajuato, as well as the very important pre-Classical centres of Chupicuaro and Michoacán, was a veritable picnic-ground for potters in pre-Columbian times.

South-eastern zone The south-eastern part of Mexico, the so-called Maya region (District IV), is a chapter unto itself. Its people played an outstanding role in pre-Columbian art. This area also includes Guatemala and Honduras, which together with the state of Chiapas in Mexico form the Maya highlands. To the south this area borders on the Pacific Ocean. The northern incline, reaching down toward the Atlantic, includes the two great river areas, Grijalva and Usumacinta, and forms the Maya lowland. This is where the main branch of the Classic Maya culture flowered. The flat and calcareous peninsula of Yucatán, bulging north-eastward far out into the Atlantic, was the setting for the last grandiose post-Classic Maya culture, which fused with the Toltec.

Mixtec plate with stylized head and the suggestion of a whispering scroll design (W. Lehmann), such as can frequently be seen in Mesoamerican illuminated manuscripts: for example, in the post-Columbian codex reproduced at the end of this volume (p. 182). It denotes that the person concerned is talking – or, in this particular case, since it is lavishly decorated, singing. We are thus dealing with a Mixtec singer. Diameter 18 cm. Private collection, Barcelona. *Cf. pp. 24, 115.*

↑

Above, left: primeval spoon with a rattle, from the central plateau of Mexico. Length 16 cm. *Above, right:* female tripod from Chupicuaro, Guanajuato. Diameter 15 cm. *Below, left:* male tripod. Diameter 17 cm. *Below, right:* bearded tripod. Diameter 15 cm. The two objects below are executed in the early style and originate from Colima. *Cf. pp. 37, 145.*

→

Black and light ware, mainly pre-Classic, from the plateau of Mexico. Height of the tallest black vase 15 cm; of the tallest light one 24 cm. *Cf. p. 38.*

Representations of the human form which, already at this early period, show an excellent under-standing for the rendering of the nude, both female and male. Middle pre-Classic; from the plateau of Mexico; Tlatilco and Tlapacoyan. Height of standing figures about 14 cm. *Cf. p. 38.*

Above, left: small monkey from Colima. Early style, which continues into the post-Classic. Actual size. *Above, right and below, left:* masks from Veracruz. Classic. *Above, right:* bearded mask with typical 'tar' painting, from Veracruz. *Below, right:* mask from Tlatilco. Middle or early pre-Classic. Actual size. *Cf. pp. 39, 40.*

↑

Cult jar. Late pre-Classic. Tlapacoyan. Height 24 cm. *Above, left:* mask. Huasteca pectoral, bearing strong resemblance to masks from the Phoenician necropolis in Cadiz. Probably also pre-Classic. Height 14 cm. *Cf. p. 40.*

← Two flutes with five flute head-pieces. *Centre:* Classic Totonac flute with suggestions of Maya style. Veracruz. Height 24 cm. *Right:* pre-Classic flute from Tlatilco. Length 32 cm. An interesting stylization of the flute as a human being, or *vice versa*. The distended body is conceived with artistic flair in all details, including the knees and feet. Note the crossed arms, which indicate an affinity with early stone sculptures from Guerrero.

Five flute head-pieces. Veracruz. Height about 5 cm. *Above, left:* markedly Negroid type. Classic. *Centre, left:* fawn-like stylization with treble flute motif and the Quetzalcóatl cross. Classic. Tuxtla area. *Below, left and right:* Semitic and white types of 'el viejo', treated in a highly realistic manner and true to life. *Centre, right:* purely Totonac hybrid type, with small beard and bird motif. Classic. *Cf. p. 40.*

IV. THE OBJECTS AND THEIR SIGNIFICANCE

Mexico, and indeed most of Mesoamerica, is still today the land of the clay pot. This brittle merchandise, produced and sold by the million all over this region, from the dustiest plazas in the smallest villages to the tile-covered market-places of ultra-modern cities, is continuously being broken and discarded in a rhythm equal to that of its production. The ocean of sherds for archaeologists to worry about in future times grows and grows. The process began more than four thousand years ago, most probably with the manufacture of useful household objects.

Household objects

PLATE P. 30

One such item of particular interest is a kind of primeval spoon, very obviously inspired by a right hand in a scooping position, the thumb still indicated in an abstract manner. The object in the spoon, the size of a modern golf ball, is a rattle, possibly used as a rhythmical instrument for religious or more frivolous dances. Alternatively it may have been a toy. Both objects were found in pre-Classic layers on the central plateau of Mexico.

One of the most widely produced clay objects was the tripod, which on account of its stability was useful for the storage of all kinds of foodstuffs, particularly those of a semi-liquid consistency. The handling of this form by the artist is an early chapter in pre-Columbian art history. Always resourceful and eager to adopt new ideas, the ancient American artist also had a remarkable ability to combine human forms with those of vessels for practical use. Three such

Above, left: female head of the 'Pretty Lady' period. Guerrero, Pacific coast. Late pre-Classic. Actual size; height 7.1 cm. Private collection. *Above, right:* Negroid head. Plateau of Mexico; Tlapacoyan. Middle pre-Classic period. Actual size; height 5.1 cm. Private collection. *Centre:* small mask of a bearded man. Pectoral, presumably from Tabasco. Pre-Classic. About actual size. Private collection. *Below, left:* head of a girl, from Veracruz. Classic period. Height 10 cm. Private collection. *Below, right:* head, from the plateau of Mexico; Tlapacoyan. About actual size; 8.5 cm. Private collection. *Cf. p. 49.*

vessels are shown in our colour plate: a female, a male, and a bearded tripod. The first is from a pre-Classic site at Chupicuaro (Guanajuato); the two others belong to the early period of Colima ware.

Not long ago (in 1963) a notable exhibition of pre-Columbian pottery was shown in Mexico City. For the first time a large number of excellent pieces was assembled from private collections and presented to the general public. All those who saw this exhibition were lost in admiration at the incredible richness and variety of the forms, as well as the extraordinary quality of these very fine ceramics.

To enter into detail about the entire wealth of ancient American pottery design would go beyond the special purpose of this book. We

PLATE P. 31

have, however, included two colour plates which will give the reader a glimpse of the natural elegant simplicity and almost modern 'line' of early pre-hispanic ceramic vessels. The upper picture shows a smart 'household service' of blackish clay, chiefly Olmec in origin, and the lower picture shows a selection of pieces in a lighter shade, including a bowl with a fish-scale design and a medium-sized ladle; both come from the plateau of Mexico.

Human representations

PLATE P. 32

The representation of human forms in fired clay is probably almost as old as pottery-making itself. However, in America interest in producing images of human beings blossomed forth in an unprecedented way, became a veritable obsession and in many cases led to a highly artistic productivity both in scope and in quality. This was the case with regard to plastic representation of the human face, as well as of the human body. Yet over-emphasis on the face is quite frequent and at times assumes rather grotesque forms, at least judged by prevalent modern standards of taste. Instances of what might be called distortion are the vivacious 'Pretty Ladies' of Guerrero, with their strangely atrophied limbs, and the classical urns of the Zapotecs. It is not without significance that still at the time of the Aztecs, who on the whole were strongly disposed toward philosophical reflection, the idea was voiced that each person was 'the owner of a face'. But the human body also was intently observed and carefully rendered. So many publications on pre-Columbian art rely exclusively on showing grim, fanatically religious sculpture, which is in its own way of great artistic merit. Certainly these works stir our artistic interest, but if only this side of the creative ability of the American artist is shown, it is no wonder that even such a well-known art historian as Sir Kenneth Clark has a false impression of early American art. It is time that the other side, the intrinsically human one, should be presented.

As well as representations of man, we find in pre-Columbian art a large proportion of animal effigies. Keen observation of nature, an *Animal effigies* outstanding and inborn trait of the ancient American approach to art, engendered some excellent results. Although this book is devoted to the investigation of human images and their artistic interpretation in the New World, I cannot resist including at least one animal representation. The plate on page 33 shows a small master- PLATE P. 33 piece, a female monkey, made by a Colima artist from the western zone (District V). With its gracious and subtle play on movement and gesture, this sculpture conveys perfectly the attitude of a coy female animal. It also expresses in an unbelievable way the inherent human side in a monkey and the monkeyish side in man!

Archaeological objects of pre-hispanic times are often referred to simply as *idolitos* in the popular Mexican idiom. There is no doubt *'Idolitos'* that with the advent of religious ideas in early times, more or less realistic idols were created in clay. They were considered as being of mystical and spiritual significance, a concept that was continuously accentuated over several millennia and finally gave its *raison d'être* to the iconographically somewhat rigid pantheon of the latest pre-Columbian epochs. Representations of deities became less and less human as time went on. They became increasingly unreal and finally were integrated with all kinds of 'magic' elements. The imagination of the sculptor was led toward the realm of the fantastic by his religious concepts and philosophic background, and often the human elements of his work almost disappeared in the symbolic aspects. But these divine creations usually had their origins in historical and human events.

One of the earliest expressions of the unreal world was the mask, *Masks* which was frequently connected with contemporary or ethnohistoric occurrences. Thus, for instance, we can detect definitely

PLATE P. 33 Semitic characteristics in a small red Tlatilco mask. The same
applies to another small mask, depicted in the same manner with

PLATE P. 36 a beard. The latter unmistakably hints at the presence of the white
man in America. The Veracruz head in the Plate on page 33 (on
the right) seems to represent a mixed Oriental type of face, with a
Mongoloid beard. The wrinkled countenance of the specimen on
the lower left expresses the pure essence of old age, a concept which
was repeated thousands of times from the earliest period onward as
the representation of the 'old' or 'fire' god.

Large masks were worn on the occasion of dances and ceremonies,
while smaller ones served as ornaments, such as pendants for neck-
laces. Dignitaries wore them as breast-plates to emphasize their
magical powers. An interesting piece from the Huasteca which served

PLATE P. 35 this function is reproduced in the Plate on page 35. It probably
comes from the pre-Classic epoch. Whistles and flutes were another
aspect of pre-hispanic art and were usually employed in rituals.

PLATE P. 34 They often exhibit very interesting details. Cult vessels proper were

PLATE P. 35 also made, as can be shown by the Plate on page 35. This con-
tainer, undoubtedly used in a ritual context, shows a magician on
one side of a typical late pre-Classic Tlapacoyan jar, with the
characteristic elongated neck. The priest, an impressive figure, is
holding a stick covered with glyphs in one hand and in the other a
bag of incense (copal), while from his head spring writhing snakes.
The body is not simply 'stuck on' to the vessel but is beautifully
integrated into its volume, emerging in high relief from the mass of
the jar.

Motives: cult If we inquire into the 'why' of all these objects, into the motives
of the dead which kindled this veritable fever of artistic activity among the
early American peoples, the answer can only be: a universal and
unshakable belief in a life after death, which found its purest expression in the deeply-rooted cult of the dead. What would Egypt
be without her tombs? What would Mexico and all of ancient
America be without the offerings for the dead found at practically
every pre-hispanic burial site? In Egypt many records were found
in cuneiform glyphs, and the wealth of written information from

Babylonia and Assyria is perhaps even greater. This material explains a great deal about the life of the ancient peoples of these lands. In early America we are in most cases dependent upon the talent of the artist for our conjectures about the way of life led by the peoples of the New World before Columbus. As from a hidden spring, a wealth of human experience gushes forth from the immense burial ground that was Mesoamerica. The objects which pious people deposited in the tombs of their fellow men are now dug out for a variety of reasons: curiosity, scholarly research and, unfortunately, greediness for money. They are taken away from the dead either carefully by archaeologists, or else brutally by treasure-hunters. There remains the consolation that the dead continue to live, although in a different way from that expected by the pious survivors. The civilized world's appreciation of the impressive achievements of the pre-hispanic artists is growing with the speed of an avalanche. Artists, connoisseurs and members of the general public are paying respectful tribute to the knowledge and vitality expressed in these works. The dead live on, in the ever-after of the world of art.

V. THE ARTIST AND HIS ORIGINS

Interpretation   The questions remain: who were these gifted people? where did they come from? These matters are increasingly becoming of vital interest. The interpretation of archaeological finds, their hypothetical explanation, is sometimes a delicate affair which many scholars dare to tackle only in a timid way, or not at all. But archaeological knowledge is gradually expanding and imposing recognition of its findings upon even hesitant investigators. The unavoidable progress of our intellectual perceptions is very well described by Peter Bamm, author of the book mentioned above, in his chapters on the 'Ribbon Ceramists' and the 'Battle-axe People' of the Sesklo-Dimini culture in the Aegean Sea area. Consider the wording of this amusing and instructive passage:

> 'Appellations, even when couched in the most objective scientific phraseology, cannot escape completely the magic of language. When confronted with the term 'Ribbon Ceramists' we willy-nilly imagine peaceful people, who seemingly delighted in adorning their pottery with exuberant variations for the joy of historical investigators. 'Battle-axe People' on the contrary immediately evokes a war-like impression. That both conceptions have gradually turned out to correspond with reality is an amusing coincidence.
>
> Viewed from the linguistic angle, a name like 'Battle-axe People' is a queer phenomenon, a solitary characteristic hanging independently, so to speak, on a branch of a prehistoric tree, like a hat on an empty hat-stand, and the task now consists of imagining the person who would fit the hat. One day, however, it comes to seem probable that the 'Battle-axe People' were Indo-Europeans. Right away the word begins to acquire an historical aura. Then it becomes known that during the period of the 'Battle-axe People' horses appear for the first time in the Aegean region. The taming of horses is a feature which

immediately arouses our sympathy. Then one finds their traces at more and more sites; thus they must be considered a widely roaming people, nomads or warriors. Each find, being a man-made object, bears intrinsically features of its creator. A ceramic pattern can be of 'abundant fantasy' or of 'sober' conception, which logically establishes that its creator either had abundant fantasy or was a sober person. With the growing amount of material the originally rather empty denominations begin to be infused with human features. The prehistoric names gradually come alive, and finally investigators speak of 'Ribbon Ceramists' and 'Battle-axe People' as other persons talk about Scandinavians or Celts.'

In ancient America the situation is no longer quite so difficult as it is in the case of the Dimini culture. In Mexico not just one but many hats are hanging on the hat-stand, as it were, belonging to a great number of very real people, whom we can identify thanks to the talent and creative will of its terracotta artists. The old fairy-tale that there was no portraiture in pre-Columbian Mexico is much mistaken. From the myriad pieces in existence one can see that a vivid portrait activity was continuously going on. Portrait sketches were realistic, fleeting, primitive, brutal, stylized, simplified, abstract, and even consisted of several components, each inspired by living faces; yet they remain portrait sketches. The strange thing is that up to now almost no one has bothered to look really closely and reflectively at these extraordinarily real human representations. It does not help when the authors of certain books simply ignore this aspect and intentionally turn their faces in the other direction. The fact is that this ancient portrait art quite obviously did exist, and fortunately provides very eloquent testimony about the early inhabitants of America. *Portraiture*

Viewed only from the physical side, we see bodies represented which are small, medium-sized, tall, fat, thin, muscular, flabby or daintily limbed; heads which are long, short or deformed; faces which are round, angular, broad or narrow; hair which is straight, kinky, shaved or even blond (not to mention the great variety of fantastic coiffures). There are eyes which are big, small, round, oval, almond- *Physical qualities*

43

shaped, slanted or slit, rising toward the temple or slanted downwards, which might indicate an ancient, inbred race in the process of degeneration. There are noses which are long and even exaggeratedly long, short, pointed, straight, curved, broad and coarse, as well as very delicate ones; there are lips that are thick, puffy, thin, straight, curved, drawn up and down at the corners, and mouths which are depicted open or closed, talking, singing, whistling, and even blowing vigorously. In short, everything is represented that humanity has produced, including ugly and ordinary as well as very beautiful people.

Expression of character

It is especially interesting to study figures of various individuals and to notice how their particular characters are expressed. We find types that are innocent or evil, intelligent or stupid, boring, lively, good-natured or malicious, sophisticated, happy, sad or content, annoyed, humorous, coy or seductive, proud, extroverted or introverted, as well as some who seem to be very wise. It is really very worth-while to dedicate some time, to muster some patience and to develop some genuine appreciation for these little terracotta creatures. One is amply rewarded for the effort by an acquaintance with this colourful crowd of different characters, of our hitherto unknown ancestors.

Racial characteristics

Furthermore, it is extremely interesting and revealing to analyse these figures with respect to their racial characteristics. At this point an unsuspected new world emerges out of the dark.

Page 45: A fine Veracruz head from the Classic period (about AD 600–800). The profile is related to that of the figure depicted on page 149, from the Staatliche Museen, Berlin-Dahlem. Another specimen which bears striking resemblance to the Berlin head is housed in the Veracruz State Museum at Jalapa. *Cf. pp. 49, 140.*

Page 46: Dead man. An impressive work of the Classic period, from Veracruz. The slight Negroid strain in this realistic representation is striking. *Cf. pp. 69, 141.*

Page 47: Small Guerrero sculptures, most of them attributable to the pre-Classic period. Of special interest is the head *(b)*, which is strongly suggestive of the Ainu, a tribe that still exists in Japan. The lack of Indian features is striking. Height: *(a)* 5 cm; *(b)* 5.6 cm; *(c)* 6.5 cm; *(d)* 5.2 cm; *(e)* 5.6 cm; *(f)* 6 cm; *(g)* 5.6 cm; *(h)* 7.5 cm; *(i)* 5.8 cm. *Cf. p. 79.*

a

b

c

d

e

f

g

h

i

Fifteen years ago, when I began an intensified study of pre-Columbian terracotta heads, I had no intention of making a study of the artistic representation of various races simply because I did not suspect that this aspect existed. On the contrary, what I was looking for were typical 'Indian' heads. It was not long, however, before I discovered that in the early, lower levels these 'genuine Indians' were not to be found. The earliest figures encountered were those with Mongoloid characteristics and also real Chinese and very Japanese wrestlers, Tartars, all kinds of white people, especially Semitic types* with and without beards, and a surprising number of Negroes and those with Negroid elements. What is considered to be genuine Indian only developed, so far as I am able to judge on the strength of these terracotta representations, in early and middle Classic times, and probably derived from earlier types. Finally came the development of a very beautiful human type, that which reached its full and adequate expression in the classical clay sculpture of the Veracruz masters.

It is clear to me that these unlooked-for results might lead to new

Non-Indian figures
PLATES PP. 36, 59

PLATE P. 45

* In recent years a considerable amount of terracottas which show characteristic Semitic traits have been found at archaeological sites. These discoveries may eventually make it obsolete to regard as mere childish nonsense certain indications in the *Book of Mormon* regarding the presence of Jewish elements in ancient America, and the definite opinions of some sixteenth- and seventeenth-century observers.

An example of the latter testimony is the chronicle of the Dominican friar, Diego Duran (born 1540 in Mexico), who dedicated the entire first chapter of his book to consideration of the possible presence of Jewish influence in pre-hispanic America. He gives substantial reasons for his opinions on the grounds of peculiarities in religious proceedings and observations on religious history. Perhaps it would be better to approach these observations with an attitude of true scientific open-mindedness than immediately to regard them as unimportant.

The same holds true for the extensive and erudite comments of Fray Gregorio García (1554–1627), also of the Dominican Order, who spent nine years in Peru and three in Mexico. He ended his career as a university professor in Spain and was a very learned man (not, as Paul Rivet implies, only seemingly so). It might be added that he knew America longer and perhaps even better than the French scholar (and in any case lived 350 years before him). Fray García's relatively little-known book, *Orígen de los Indios del Nuevo Mundo*, must definitely be considered a document of primary historical importance written by an intellectually

Further specimens of small Guerrero sculptures in which different ethnic elements are emphasized. *Centre:* the two heads *(b)* and *(e)* are very early Negroid renderings from the southern part of Mexico. Height: *(a)* 5 cm; *(b)* 5 cm; *(c)* 4.5 cm; *(d)* 7 cm; *(e)* 7 cm; *(f)* 8 cm; *(g)* 7 cm; *(h)* 5 cm; *(i)* 7 cm. *Cf. p. 9.*

perspectives concerning our knowledge of certain ethno-historical events and population migrations. Because the individual and racial characteristics of the human face are something that no one would be able to invent by accident, it seems to me that if ever anything were created by God, it was surely the racial differentiations of mankind. It is in contradiction, moreover, to the most elementary logic and to all artistic experience that an Indian could depict in a masterly way the head of a Negro or of a white person without missing a single racial characteristic, unless he had actually seen *Racial* such a person. The types of people they depicted must have lived *intermingling* in America and most probably propagated because, as has been strikingly observed, 'when two different populations meet they may become friends or enemies, but they always breed!' We are thus faced with the fact that very early population units in the Meso-american region were exposed to intensive and varied racial inter-mingling. It is here that the genuine 'melting-pot' of America can be found, not in North America, where mixing has taken place in

disciplined eye-witness. The first edition was published in 1607 but apparently fell victim to the censorship of the Spanish Inquisition in Mexico, which explains to some degree the peculiar silence about the book and its author in all Mexican sources. Fortunately the work was republished in Madrid in 1729. In any case, the high purposes of true scientific research would be better served if in future one could avoid the trenchant and cocksure 'no' and the condescending smiles which appear when some of these questions are raised.

Another report, presented at the International Congress of Americanists in Barcelona in 1964, merits objective attention. This paper, given by Miss Henriette Mertz, an American lawyer and oceanographer, claims that it was historically possible for Ulysses to have voyaged into American waters. Novel trains of thought should not be rejected without valid reason, even if at first glance they deal with hypotheses hitherto unacceptable in anthropological circles. I am convinced that there will be many a surprise coming our way in the next ten years, when more of the inexhaustible wealth of American archaeological material has been excavated and studied.

One such surprise is the very recently found little clay fragment from Tlatilco (a bearded head 4 cm high), which is incredibly similar to old Greek and Phoenician items and forms a worthy counterpart to the

PLATES PP. 164,
165

PLATE P. 181

FIG. I

magnificent Guatemalan incense-burner of the Musée de l'Homme in Paris. Even more startling is the discovery of a kind of Negroid Silenus mask, made by an Olmec master and also stemming from Tlatilco, as I was informed by a competent authority; this appears on page 181 (Figure d).

To this category also belongs the small terracotta head which the Mexican archaeologist, José García Payón, excavated in 1933 inside the pyramid of Calixtlahuaca, near Toluca, and which according to the judgment of Professor Boehringer from Germany should be classed typologically with Roman works of about 200 AD. This and many other finds are beginning to demand, in an ever more pressing way, a scientific explanation. (See *Bulletin of the Mexican Institute of Anthropology*, No. 6, October 1961.)

FIG. 1 – *So-called 'Roman' head, excavated in the pyramid of Calixtlahuaca. Approx. 2nd cent. AD. After an original photograph by Baron J. Hennet in Mexico City.*

much more recent times (leaving many problems unsolved because of its inconclusive nature).

The next question that logically arises is: where did all these people come from? Did they slowly evolve from genes already in existence from remotest antiquity? Did they migrate sooner or later in the normal manner, with the main stock of aborigines *via* the Bering Strait?

Or did they after all arrive from somewhere else? During the International Congress of Americanists in Mexico City in 1962, the high point of discussion was reached with the debate between the so-called 'diffusionists' and the 'anti-diffusionists', that is, between scholars who are of the opinion that long before the time of Columbus trans-oceanic contacts with America were possible, probable or even certain; and those who deny on principle any possibility of such contacts.

The theory of all diffusionists is based on study and comparison of innumerable elements which appeared simultaneously in different parts of the world. In this respect the extensive contribution of Dr. Alfonso Caso to the above-mentioned congress was very instructive.*

Diffusionist theory

On the matter of cultural diffusion I agree with Dr. Caso in many respects, without going so far as to reject the usefulness of a minute study of details in this field. Nevertheless for methodological reasons his warning is thoroughly understandable and should be taken into consideration, especially with respect to artistic activities. The simultaneous appearance of decorative designs should be given relatively little weight in proving the diffusionist theory. The instructive confrontation in Dr. Caso's selection of decorative patterns, which run from a ring from Mycenae to a detail on a Louis XVI table in

* *Actas y Memorias del XXXV Congreso Internacional de Americanistas*, vol. I, pp. 55 ff.

FIGS. 2, 3 – *Left: pre-Classic head from Monte Albán. Right: Neolithic object, Palestine. (Congress Papers, Fig. 6.)*

the Louvre, was amusing, well-chosen and to the point. One might also admit to the strong possibility of doubt in the simultaneous appearance of mythological ideas, glyphs, idiomatic peculiarities etc.

'Faciology'

The case is quite different, in my opinion, when we enter upon the comparison of human representations, especially of human faces —a study which, in my paper at the International Congress of Americanists in Barcelona (1964), I proposed should be called 'faciology'. In this sphere, more fundamental and of deeper significance, it seems to me that the chance of coincidental invention is almost non-existent, even when one considers the problems of geographical separation. To be sure, one must be very careful when making these comparisons. The sample employed by Caso in his

Old World parallels

afore-mentioned lecture (Figure 8, Congress Report), a Merovingian sculpture from Ratisbon and the double-bearded terracotta head from the Balsas region of Guerrero, was not well chosen. The two pieces are only related in their exterior aspects, whereas their essential characteristics are quite different. The sculpture from Ratisbon shows an ancient Germanic personality, while the terra-

Very early representations from Guerrero which probably belong to the early pre-Classic period, called by me the 'goggle-eye' type; they already give proof of a certain sense of style. *(g)* is the only whole figure of this kind so far known. It forms part of the private collection of Dr. Leof in Mexico City. Height: *(a)* 5.6 cm; *(b)* 4.9 cm; *(c)* 5 cm; *(d)* 6 cm; *(e)* 5.5 cm; *(f)* 5.5 cm; *(g)* 17 cm. *Cf. p. 79.*

b

d

f

g

cotta head from Guerrero is quite obviously what might be considered an outlandish, grotesque deity, namely the god Bes, who was well known in Egypt and of whom terracotta images appear at practically all Phoenician excavation sites bordering the Mediterranean.* In comparing such objects only the intrinsic essence of the artistic concept should be taken into consideration and not merely their superficial, exterior similarities.

Extremely well chosen, on the contrary, are the samples of Figures 6 and 7 (Congress Report), because here we see the same fundamental concept at work in the two juxtaposed subjects. Figure 6 compares a pre-Classic head from Monte Albán, Oaxaca, with a Neolithic figure found in Palestine; both were found at an Archaic level but are unquestionably identical so far as their sculptural form and expression are concerned. Still more astonishing, because they were found at a higher level, are the results of a comparison of a well-known stone relief disc from Veracruz, depicting a bearded man, with the head of an Etruscan funeral figure. Accidental inventiveness on two different continents…? Perhaps only God knows how close Alfonso Caso came to the truth (still hidden to us) with the two comparisons, although they were included in the essay of this Mexican anthropologist to prove a different point.

* I am indebted to the well-known German sinologist, Professor Hintze of Darmstadt, for confirming the 'Bes' character of the Guerrero head and also for drawing my attention to the fact that similar representations have been found in the Altai mountains of Russia.

Four pre-Classic 'dignitaries'. Guerrero, coastal area. These figures may be compared with similar terracottas from Baluchistan. *Cf. p. 80.*

A strange and often tense atmosphere usually prevails as soon as the burning question of diffusion is touched upon, which in my opinion stands in need of a serious, intense and above all objective study. One should not be too nervous about the problem and above all should not try systematically to suppress the free play of rival tendencies in research, as sometimes seems to be the case even at universities. Neither comical entertaining books like the one recently written by the renowned professor of Tulane University, Robert Wauchope, nor one-sided polemical treatises usually composed by rather passionate advocates of contact theories are likely to solve the riddle of American population history, which continues to exist, as the leading ethnological expert, Paul Rivet, is forced to admit in his latest book.

Nevertheless, every case of serious interest in this question may in the end gradually lead to a better understanding of what really took place. It is worth while to examine the smallest details and to compare them in all directions, even if they afford only weak clues, circumstantial and supplementary items perhaps, to the entire many-faceted mosaic. The reason is that weak clues are better than none in attempting to explain, in all this cultural and ethnological diversity, coincidental developments in pre-Columbian America that are otherwise incomprehensible and often more than surprising. With the annual increase in the amount of archaeological finds and in more complete knowledge of excavated material it is becoming less and less likely that there were no contacts whatsoever between America and the rest of the world in early times. The illustrative material in this book likewise seems to point in this direction in a quite obvious way.

FIG. 5 – *Head of an Etruscan funerary figure. (Congress Papers, Fig. 7.)*

B. THE ARTISTIC ACHIEVEMENT

Group of Semitic types. Provenance (from left to right): Guerrero, Veracruz, Tlatilco, Maya (incense-burner), Nayarit (fragment), Chiapas (mask). Pre-Classic, except the Nayarit figurine. Height of Guerrero head 13.5 cm; of Chiapas head 14 cm. *Cf. p. 49.*

A pregnant girl, represented with natural simplicity and grace. Classic. Veracruz. Height 19 cm. *Cf. p. 67.*

Enigmatic heads of men of different races. From the pre-Classic period at Guerrero. The head *above*, *right* was discovered in the sierra above Petatlán, the others at Tecpan de Galeana. Actual sizes. *Cf. pp. 75, 76.*

Pre-Classic figures from Guerrero, calling to mind archaic Japanese terracottas. The complete figure is a unique specimen in the Josué Saenz Collection in Mexico City. All figures are about actual size. *Cf. p. 81.*

Heads in *pastillage* technique from the Pacific coast of Guerrero. About 500 BC. *Top row*, from left to right: persons wearing turbans. Height: 7 cm, 10 cm, 9 cm. *Centre row*, from left to right. Height: 6.5 cm, 9 cm, 10.5 cm. *Bottom row*, from left to right: late period. Height: 7 cm, 8 cm, 6 cm, 8 cm. *Cf. p. 87.*

'Pretty Lady' type of the late pre-Classic period, from Guerrero. The bust of this elegant, highly cultured lady *(left)* is here slightly enlarged (actual size 14 cm). The heads *(right)* measure in height, from top to bottom, 5 cm, 8 cm and 5 cm. The lowest, which possesses an uncommon vitality, is not from the coast but from the sierra of Guerrero. *Cf. p. 87.*

Above: 'flat faces' from Guerrero, showing the development from the primitive stage to the Classic period. Height of object on the left 9.5 cm; of that on the right 8 cm. *Below:* representations in stone from Guerrero. *Left:* 'Chontale' mask from the Taxco area, emulating in stone the technique used for modelling in clay. Height 15 cm. *Centre:* Classic mask executed in a highly stylized linear technique, which may have exerted an influence upon subsequent post-Classic Mixtec gem-cutters. Height 8.5 cm. *Right:* typical Mexala figurine, derived from the shape of an axe. Height 12 cm. *Cf. p. 93.*

Page 65: Further examples of 'Pretty Lady' heads. Late pre-Classic, from the Pacific coast of Guerrero. These six elegant girls, with bold hairstyles and lively facial expressions, are here reproduced in their actual size. *Cf. p. 87.*

The human drive for self-expression can adopt very different forms, which depend not only upon the stage of general evolution of the culture concerned, but also upon the concentrated energies of a single creative individual. For a long time we have called these single-minded individuals artists. The greater the difficulties which confront this special kind of person, the stronger, the more over-powering and the more unique are often their achievements. Pre-cisely during the relatively primitive stages of the evolution of humanity, an almost explosive character appears quite frequently in artistic creations. It carries within itself the strength to overwhelm all obstacles, and also possesses the capacity to act as a kind of original seed, engendering, directing and ushering in the beginning of a whole sequence of developments. Then and only then do we speak of genuine Archaic art.

Archaic art

Mexico especially is overflowing with examples bearing witness to this kind of art which, for ever renewing itself, permeates the whole region of Mesoamerica like a series of rivulets. It is then only a question of time, of local geographical influences and of the ex-tremely complicated human relationships already mentioned, which affect the flow of the streams and divert their paths from the austere, powerful source into calmer channels of seasoned and mature cre-ativity. Sometimes this procedure develops quietly and naturally, sometimes unsteadily with continual interruptions by counter-in-fluences.

The period of maturity, which corresponds more or less with our concept of the Classic epoch, is practically without exception suc-ceeded by a late art, which can also be very attractive and may not be inferior in quality to the art of other periods. However, in most cases it contains the germ of degeneration and inevitable decay.

In all stages of this art, as has been said before, the representation of man plays an important role with regard to both the depiction

PLATE P. 60

67

FIG. 6 – *Egyptian representation showing prisoners of different ethnic composition. From the temple of Ptah at Memphis. XIXth Dynasty (Ramses II), approx. 1200 BC.*

of the face and the shaping of the body. Naturally this holds true for the works of almost all peoples, although fundamentally different concepts may be involved. Thus, for instance, the hierarchic, stiff and unapproachable attitude dominated in Mesopotamia, slightly awkward but sturdy reality with the Hittites, unrivalled idealization of the body with the Greeks, the free gesture of movement with the Carthaginians and Sardinians, and private intimacy transmuted from real life with the Etruscans. Only rarely do we find that the same people develop a far-reaching and amply conceived versatility in the artistic handling of human representations, as in Egypt, where the bodies were certainly never freed from stylistic fetters, but where, in contrast, the representation of the face, i.e. portraiture in the wider sense of the word, reached a high level of expressiveness. The characteristics of portraiture at times invaded even representations of sacrosanct and semi-divine rulers. They profoundly enhanced portraits of public officers and reached a remarkable stage in subtle, yet sharp observation in the characterization of foreign prisoners – precisely those persons in the most unfortunate circumstances.

Pre-Columbian and Egyptian art

When we look at the very varied range of human representations featured in pre-Columbian art, it is perhaps only in Egypt that we find certain points of valid comparison. In ancient America the subject of man has been handled in a possibly less grandiose way than on the Nile; nevertheless its interpretations are more diversified

FIG. 6

in their ramifications, of more abundant fantasy and of more lively, unexpected variety. This phenomenon can be seen in all regions of Mesoamerica and in all stages of development of its art, from the most primitive to the most mature, from the creation of purest abstractions and wilful stylizations to the superb achievements of an accomplished artistic realism. There is no other art in the world which has presented us with such a manifold variety of expressions. Hitherto we simply have not known enough about it or have not looked at it with enough understanding and sensitive empathy.

In a recently published book, *Art before Columbus*, the American author, André Emmerich, voices the opinion (a highly justified complaint) that this fantastic branch of human creative skill is mostly non-existent even in the large art museums of the world. Thirty years ago I discussed this omission with the Curator of the Print Department of the Metropolitan Museum in New York. The gentleman in question, whose department included the museum's magnificent Dürer Collection, seemed to consider me almost a half-wit. He told me quite apodictically that pre-Columbian 'stuff' had no place whatsoever in a real art museum. Slightly annoyed, I drew his attention to the well-known remarks of Albrecht Dürer in the Netherland Diary about the first American 'art exhibition' in Europe, at Brussels in 1520. Sigvald Linné cites the Dürer text verbatim in the first volume on ancient America in the ART OF THE WORLD series; for one of the earliest mentions of the text the reader is referred to Pál Kelemen's *Medieval American Art* (1947), a modern appreciation of pre-Columbian art. *[Dürer on pre-Columbian art]*

The Dürer text testifies to the spontaneous and genuine admiration of the great German master for the objects which had just arrived from the New World, sent by Cortés to Emperor Charles V, who was residing at that time in the Netherlands. My reference to this historical document was completely lost on the elderly Curator, who apparently did not care to make any effort whatsoever to revise his preconceived opinion on the subject of my beloved pre-Columbian art. My departure from his office took place in an atmosphere of extreme coolness on both sides.

In the last thirty years, to be sure, a fundamental change in the *[Present-day attitudes]* general attitude has taken place. Yet the fact remains, as Emmerich points out, that in most countries splendid creations of pre-Columbian art are half-hidden in overcrowded show-cases, or are kept completely out of sight in the storerooms of ethnographic institutions, or else are ensconced in private collections, often difficult of access to the general public. Certain recent events will probably help to accelerate the trend toward greater appreciation of pre-Columbian art. The vast Mexican Exhibition which travelled to many countries paved the way, and the placement of the Robert Wood-Bliss Collection in an appropriate building in Washington, D.C., as well as the inauguration of the stupendous new Anthropology Museum in Mexico City and the Diego Rivera Museum (Anahuacalli) on its outskirts, will figure as landmarks in this direction.

Olmec figures from Guerrero. *(a)*, *(d)*: the earliest representations of wrestlers in pre-Columbian art. About 1800 BC. Pacific coast. Height: *(a)* 10 cm; *(d)* 7 cm. *(b)*, *(c)*: early heads which illustrate the way in which the style developed. Height: *(b)* 6.5 cm; *(c)* 6 cm. *Below, centre (g)*: a fully developed Olmec terracotta in the Josué Saenz Collection, Mexico City. *(e)* is a distinctly naturalistic rendering of an Olmec boy which is also typical of the finds made in Morelos. Height: 5 cm. *(f)*, *(i)*: later renderings in kaolin which demonstrate the interplay between the vertical style favoured by the white elements in Guerrero and the refined art and greater technical perfection of the Olmecs. Height of *(h)*, *(f)* and *(i)*: 6 cm. They originate from the border area between Guerrero and Puebla. *Cf. p. 81.*

a

b

c

C. FIGURATIVE REPRESENTATIONS IN
THE VARIOUS REGIONS OF MEXICO

Early 'Semitic' type from Guerrero, Pacific coast. All these figures were used to ornament incense-burners — or more correctly, as essential elements in their design. The lively dynamism of this primitive early art is astonishing. Height: *(a)* 14 cm; *(b)* 12 cm; *(c)* 9.7 cm and 9 cm. *Cf. p. 86.*

I. THE SOUTH: GUERRERO AND MORELOS

Especially in the south, and chiefly in Guerrero, archaeological discoveries emerge from time to time which have no connection whatsoever or very little in common with those of other pre-Columbian cultures. Famous in this respect is the small double-bearded terracotta head which was found in the Balsas River district, and which we now recognize without any doubt as a representation of the Phoenician and Egyptian deity, Bes. Thirty years ago this piece, *FIG. 7* housed in the Museum of Natural History in New York, so greatly puzzled the Director, George Vaillant, with whom I repeatedly discussed the problems of early Mexican ceramics, that it led him to write an essay on bearded representations in pre-Columbian art. If this meritorious American archaeologist were still alive, he would certainly be astonished to see all the similar enigmatic figures which in the meantime have joined the 'Bearded Man' from Balsas. I call these rather indefinable solitary individuals, in default of a better *FIG. 7* name, the *Urweisse* ('Ancient Whites') of Guerrero, first because *'Ancient Whites'* from the racial point of view they seem to belong more to the white species of mankind than to any other, and secondly because many of them, though perhaps not all, might even be considered pre-Olmec (almost 400 years old) – a point of view shared by other connoisseurs of the Guerrero finds.

In every investigation the question naturally arises: where can the *Oldest works in* beginning of all human representations be found? Very often visitors *Guerrero* to my private collection ask which piece I would consider to be hypothetically the oldest. Usually I point to the head shown in the upper left corner of the Plate on page 61, which I call 'Tecpan Man' on *PLATE P. 61* account of the fact that it was discovered at Tecpan de Galeana, 90 kilometres north of Acapulco. The vigorously modelled face with its wide forehead and broad chin reminds me of a human being which derived originally from ancestors with Cro-Magnon skulls.

Also of exceptional interest are the figures reproduced beside 'Tec- *PLATE P. 61*

FIG. 7 – *Bearded terracotta head from the Balsas River area of Guerrero, undoubtedly representing the Phoenician deity Bes. Actual size. Drawing after a photograph kindly supplied by Dr. Gordon Eckholm. Original in the Natural History Museum, New York.*

LOWER LEFT

PLATE P. 61

PLATE P. 61
LOWER RIGHT

pan Man'. The bearded person with a cloth hanging down on the right side of his head looks like a Hittite or a Persian. This diminutive piece, only 6 centimetres high, was found quite recently in an excavation made for a new school in Tecpan, almost 4 metres below the surface. In spite of its slightly decomposed and washed-out state, it still radiates a certain dignity and can be considered a minor but well-composed achievement. A tiny head 3 centimetres high, shown in the centre of the Plate on page 61, has a very distinguished profile. Due to the round head deformation, it gives the impression that the person is wearing a fez. Viewed from the back, however, the cranial deformation is clearly visible.

The representative of the white race reproduced in the upper right corner was not found, as was the case with his other colleagues, near the Pacific coast at Tecpan but further inland. A clearly discernible feature and the pre-Classic 'A' type eyes, which consequently suggest a fairly definite chronological classification. Quite remarkable are the opulent moustache and the peculiar head-dress, which give a rather bizarre appearance to this bearded individual, who is otherwise realistically represented. The last head is a little gem of early Mexican clay sculpture. It depicts impressively the strong character of a self-reliant personage, undoubtedly disposed in his lifetime to command rather than to obey orders. It is almost uncanny to see how the artist managed to show with unerring skill

Pre-Classic heads from the Pacific coast of Guerrero (about 500 BC), executed in the so-called *pastillage* style and wearing a very lively expression. Whereas most renderings depict the white element, head *(e)* is a fine example of the Olmec strain in this early people of southern Mexico. Height: *(a)* 9.8 cm; *(b)* 11 cm; *(c)* 11 cm; *(d)* 11.5 cm; *(e)* 10.5 cm; *(f)* 11.5 cm. *Cf. p. 87.*

76

a

b

c

d

the penetrating look and the concentrated energy of this natural leader of ancient times. This piece was also found at Tecpan and shows an easily discernible Olmec influence. The clay has acquired through petrification the hardness and consistency of stone.

There is great variety among our strange guests from the southern part of Guerrero. In the Plate on page 47 I have combined some PLATE P. 47 especially interesting samples. Each of these heads embodies a world of its own and is aesthetically and ethnologically quite important. Examining these pieces, one cannot help but have a peculiar feeling with respect to the truth about the early history of the population of the New World. I leave it to the reader to contemplate this hitherto unpublished material and make his own judgment. I personally have not been able to discover among these distinguished personages a single 'real Indian'.

The bearded face in the centre of the upper row on page 47 is ex- PLATE P. 47 tremely rare. It shows precisely the characteristics of an Ainu. This tribe, which still inhabits the northern part of Japan and is of Caucasian origin, could have migrated to America *via* the Bering Strait. The two Negroid heads on page 48 are quite conspicuous. PLATE P. 48 They prove that this racial type can be found nearly everywhere in ancient America, if only in small numbers and in isolated instances. Much the same can be said about the next group, which PLATE P. 53 probably also made its first appearance in very remote times on the Pacific coast of Guerrero and the Costa Chica of Oaxaca. Due to their peculiar and easily recognizable eye technique, incised and protruding, which results in a rather fierce look, I have classified this species independently as the 'goggle eye' type. In spite of their PLATE P. 53 unquestionable stylization, they have a very vital and realistic expression.

Representations of the 'Pretty Ladies', from the Pacific coast of Guerrero. *(a)* has a fine head-dress and tattooing which forms an artful 'S'-shaped line around the breasts. Height 12 cm. *(b)* has an unmistakable accentuation of the female characteristics and large round eyes executed in the style of San Jerómino, Guerrero. Height 11 cm. *(c)* is a delightfully conceived pregnant woman. Height about 14 cm. *(d)*: a particularly elegant girl who can hardly have been an 'Indian'. Height about 10 cm. Private collection, Paris. *Cf. p. 87.*

PLATE P. 53 On page 53 we see an array of figures which seem to belong to the white race, although an early Negroid element can also be spotted. The two bearded heads, A and B, imbued with a sort of Aegean dignity, actually remind us of pre-Hellenic representations. The PLATE P. 54 four great dignitaries of the New World on page 54 are wearing richly adorned headbands and have a slightly forbidding look. They represent unequivocally the hieratic element in the colourful magic world of Guerrero. The one depicted in the upper left corner is carrying an owl on the right side of his naked torso.

In comparison with the previous pictures, the next figures seem to PLATE P. 62 be inconsistent. Yet they also belong to the rich and varied pattern of human life in ancient Guerrero. The description of the oldest terracottas found in Guerrero would not be complete without mention of those pieces which in certain respects remind us of ancient *Japanese* Japanese ceramics, Jōmon and Haniwa. Very surprising is the simi-
parallels larity between the archaic 'slit-up' figures, which according to Emmerich could be from the very earliest period, and some Jōmon pieces recently published by E. Kidder (October 1964). An ex-
REVERSE OF tremely primitive but powerfully modelled specimen of this type
SLIP-CASE from Guerrero is shown on the back of the slip-case of this book. The terracottas of Japan are more stylized but feature clearly the same frontal cut, which begins below the chin and usually reaches to a point below the belly. Neither the exact date nor the real significance of these 'slit-up' bodies (sometimes depicted in a highly realistic way in Mexico) is known to us. Caesarean section has even been suggested, because until recently only female representations of this type had been found. But newer discoveries of male figures havo also been made in Guerrero. They are of extremely brutal but aesthetically interesting workmanship. From this we might assume that symbolic or actual human sacrifice was practised. The locations where these pieces are found extend from Zihuatanejo (Weitlander-Barlow Expedition) to the upper Balsas River and a little farther inland. So far as I know, their appearance is restricted only to the above-mentioned area of Guerrero. The specimen on display in the Musée de l'Homme in Paris among contemporary Otomi folk art may have been found in an Otomi region but is probably an object

that was taken there from elsewhere and is now accidentally mis-placed.

Other terracottas which strongly remind us of archaic Japanese pieces are shown in the Plate on page 62, and come from the Pacific coast. An exceptionally beautiful piece, almost classic in its simplicity, is the very rare whole figure in the private collection of Josué Saenz. All these strange finds made in Guerrero deserve to attract greater interest on account of the latest research by the American anthropologist, Clifford Evans, of the Smithsonian Insti-tute in Washington, made public at the International Congress of Americanists in Spain in 1964. His diggings on the west coast of Ecuador seem to prove fairly conclusively that the oldest ceramic sherds ever found on American soil (the approximate date of 3000 BC was mentioned) coincide with similar pottery of the archaic Jōmon period in Japan. Dr. Evans, who adheres to the theory of trans-Pacific contacts, also admitted the possibility of landings on the Pacific coast of Guerrero due to certain prevailing ocean currents. The excavations of Ellen and Charles Brush in Puerto Marquez, mentioned earlier in this book, corroborate the observations and evidence of Evans, since at the lowest level of their diggings sherds were found which also bear a similarity to early Japanese ware.

Later in this book we will have the opportunity to compare pieces from the cultures of Esmeraldas and Manabí, Ecuador, which in so far as they extend into the southern part of western Colombia are called 'Tumaco'. We also find in western Colombia figures of the Chibcha culture, which are of later manufacture and resemble the 'Japanese' heads from Guerrero. It may be that here also a fossili-zation of archaic styles took place similar to that which occurred in the western part of Mexico.

It seems to me that further more precise investigations might in future connect the above-mentioned finds with the still very problem-atic matter of the Olmecs. The very oldest creations of the Olmecs, already stylistically recognizable, are undoubtedly those from the Pacific coast of Guerrero in the form of primitive clay sculptures. These belong stratigraphically and typologically, according to the Puerto Marquez excavations, to the early pre-Classic epoch. The

PLATE P. 62

Trans-Pacific contact and the Olmec problem

PLATE P. 71

unmistakably rounded, moulded form of face and body is an interesting point, as well as the fact that here wrestlers make their first appearance. In much later times the expression of this subject reached its zenith in the famous 'La Venta' sculpture in the National Museum of Anthropology in Mexico City. In these figurines the typical Olmec face with the turned-down corners of the mouth can be observed, as well as other stylistic peculiarities which eventually formed the basis for a much more simplified symbolism. In the last and most sophisticated phases of Olmec culture the stylistic, aesthetic process led to a highly refined abstract art.

Apart from the primitive figures soon to make their appearance there are representations of human faces, occasionally quite realistic and giving us a very clear idea of what the Olmecs looked like. They are sometimes less 'Asiatic', perhaps in some instances already mixed with the original white population (*Urweisse*), and can be found not only in the south proper but also in the state of Morelos, which borders Guerrero on the north. This area has given us, apart from the well-known great stone reliefs of Chalcatzingo, which are already of a stylistically higher developed epoch, the pre-Classic 'Baby Face' types from Gualupita. Also from Morelos at Atlihuaján comes the especially interesting clay sculpture of an Olmec with a highly-stylized jaguar skin on his back.

How the Olmecs managed to get to America to begin with, *via* the Bering Strait or by trans-Pacific contacts, is still an open question. But the fact that they were there, and also the fact that precisely in Guerrero we find all nuances of Olmec art, are absolutely certain. The whole scale of forms, from the most primitive to the most PLATE P. 71 sophisticated and refined, is amply represented in this southern region.

The well-known Mexican archaeologist, Roman Piña Chán, and

Six Negroid heads: *(a)*, *(c)*, *(f)* from Tlatilco; *(b)* from Tabasco; *(d)* from Chiapas; *(e)* and *(g)* from Guerrero; *(h)* and *(i)* from the central plateau of Mexico. *(e)* is a clay sculpture of particular beauty, which combines the Negroid element with the vertical tendency of the Guerrero coastal style. Height: *(a)* 4.5 cm; *(b)* 4.5 cm; *(c)* 5 cm; *(d)* 6.5 cm; *(e)* 7 cm; *(f)* 4.5 cm; *(g)* 6 cm; *(h)* 5 cm; *(i)* 6 cm. *Cf. p. 95.*

b

c

e

f

h

i

Luís Covarrubias, a brother of the outstanding investigator and writer, the late Miguel Covarrubias, published in 1964 an interesting book about the Olmecs entitled *The People of the Jaguar*. In this work the extraordinary tendency toward stylization in the art of these people has been traced and described well. In addition to some excellent photographs illustrating Olmec art treasures, a considerable number of fine drawings by Miguel Covarrubias have been included, which unfortunately do not always indicate the origin of the piece concerned. In these drawings, however, the essential concepts followed by the Olmec masters in depicting racial features are well indicated.

In the conclusions of this work it is especially emphasized that the Olmec culture definitely originated in the region of La Venta; however, I am of a different opinion. All the latest radiocarbon tests of sites yielding Olmec material have been carefully arranged in a highly meritorious way, but in my opinion these dates demonstrate exactly the contrary of what the authors try to prove. The farther we advance toward the south-west, and certainly *not* toward the east (Tabasco), the older the radiocarbon dates become, and this is particularly so when we begin to approach the Pacific coast. In Valdivia (Ecuador) the dates (so far as they are known) go back to 2393–2093 BC at the earliest; in Panama (Monagrillo phase) to 2130 BC; in Guatemala, Morelos and Tlatilco to 1500–1000 or 800 BC; and in La Venta to 1154–174 BC. It seems incomprehensible to me that the highly significant dates established by the excavation of Ellen and Charles Brush at Puerto Marquez, Guerrero, have not been taken into consideration, although they are quite close to the dates for Valdivia and Panama and would have fitted very well into the above arrangement. It is unfortunate that the valuable contribution of Mr and Mrs Brush, which was publicly read by Mrs

Origins of Olmecs

Interesting twin figures from the lid of a funerary urn, found recently on the border between Guerrero and Michoacán. This style, hitherto unknown, probably belongs to the late Classic or early post-Classic period and may be Proto-Toltec in origin. Height 27 cm. *Cf. p. 102.*

85

Brush at the XXXV Congress of Americanists in Mexico City in 1964, was not included in the official report of the Congress but only mentioned in a few lines. In the new Skira publication by Professor Lothrop the pre-Columbian art of Guerrero was hardly mentioned at all and then only in a few brief lines, in spite of the fact that the famous American archaeologist, Matthew Stirling, had drawn the attention of the Convention of the American Archaeological Association (held in Mexico City in 1959) to the importance of the Olmec finds in Guerrero, recommending more intensive research in this area (apparently without much response). Therefore I have presented this southern region of Mexico in greater detail, relying on my modest experience and research, to enable the reader to become a little better acquainted with this hitherto almost unknown but archaeologically very important material, which can also claim great artistic significance.

PLATE P. 72
*Semitic figures
from Guerrero*

For the sake of presenting a comprehensive picture, I have also dedicated a special black-and-white plate to the Semitic figures from Guerrero, who also dwelt there on the Pacific coast in early times, chiefly in the neighbourhood of Acapulco, and probably in considerable numbers. The items shown are clay heads attached to ceramic vessels, which, I am fairly certain, were used as incense-burners. The accomplished ethnologist and Director of the Milwaukee Museum, Stephan Borhegyi, discovered such vessels in Guatemala and has compared them with similar ones from ancient Palestine. Stylistically they do not coincide with the 'goggle eye' type from Guerrero, which hardly ever showed Semitic characteristics. Yet there may have been a loose connection between the two styles.

The curious points about these essentially primitive figures are that, first, there is an emphasis on markedly Semitic-Hebrew features, sometimes very dignified and in other cases conveying an effect of caricature; second, the invariable presentation of these persons, probably priests, with high hats; third, an elongated groove on the back of the heads; and fourth, the fact that all of them without exception were depicted as crying, i.e., with incised lines running down from the eyes, over both cheeks. In some cases even the rolling tears were indicated. The meaning of this we do not know. Even an approximately exact classification is very difficult. Perhaps they may be connected with the later 'flat faces' which we shall treat in another section.

We know a little more about the heads executed in the so-called *pastillage* technique described earlier. According to the Brush excavation, they appeared around the middle of the first millennium BC and apparently continued to evolve during the whole late pre-Classic epoch. The treatment of the features of this group is one of the most interesting chapters of Guerrero ceramics. First, they give the impression that all types of white men were known; second, the sculptures achieve a highly artistic effect by employing one of the most primitive techniques known to us; and third, the refined works of this last period constitute the quite extraordinary creation of a late stylistic development. The concept of the human head in a triangular prismatic shape is unique, combined with vertical over-elongation of a most sophisticated kind.

PLATES PP. 63, 77

PLATE P. 77

Equally interesting is the immediately following phase of the 'Pretty Ladies' of Guerrero. Again we seem to be confronted by representatives of the white race. The incision technique of the eyes, it is true, is quite different from that of the preceding period; yet the striking vertical tendency is carried over, producing a special effect one might even call a fashionable eloquence. These enchanting females have a generally elegant bearing and poise, delicately drawn (or plucked) eyebrows and small mouths, opulent coiffures and artistic finery, and, surpassing everything else, an extremely vivacious look in their eyes.

'*Pretty Ladies*'
PLATES PP. 64,
65, 78

There is no doubt that up to now the clay sculptures of Guerrero have been considered as stepchildren and have been completely neglected by archaeological investigators. Slightly better known (if only in recent times) are the stone artifacts so typical of this southern region. In this regard the exhibition of Guerrero stone sculpture, organized in 1964 by the National University of Mexico, served to open the eyes of many visitors to Mexico who are interested in pre-Columbian art. The powerful impact, the subtle simplicity and refined 'modern' feeling of these superb works were very ably demonstrated. Unfortunately their creators are still practically unknown to us.*

One of the remarkable things about this art is the repetitious duality of two groups, one of which developed directly from the stone axe and occurs in a great variety of anthropomorphic representations. This group of works is usually attributed to the Mexcala culture, for the reason that its main site is near Mexcala on the middle reaches of the Balsas River. The second group did not derive from the stone axe but quite obviously goes back to imitations of PLATE P. 66 clay sculptures logically from an earlier period. Whereas the oldest specimens of the first group might even belong to a pre-ceramic epoch, the works in the second group would fit into the late pre-Classic period. Both groups, however, seem to have existed for a long time thereafter in Guerrero. The great craftsmanship of the southern stone-cutters and of their stone sculptures was well known until the Aztec era and has appeared again even in recent times. Innumerable copies of old stone pieces and some competent new creations by Guerrero artists ably demonstrate this.

On the whole, Guerrero can be considered as a kind of whirlpool of all the different pre-Columbian cultures. In addition to the above-mentioned two major groups, superb Olmec stone works of all stages of development were produced. Later, during the Classic era, *Teotihuacán works* the 'provincial' Teotihuacán stone masks and figures were fairly *in Guerrero* prominent. However, I am not absolutely sure that the so-called 'provincial' stone sculptures have to be interpreted as reflexes inspired by the works made at the great central shrine of Teotihuacán. On the contrary, the possibility also exists that Teotihuacán art might have been influenced by that of Guerrero. In this respect the fact should be mentioned that a great number of small clay figurines have been found in the vicinity of the Pacific coast

---

* An illuminating book on the stonework of Guerrero is now being prepared by the excellent connoisseur of the art of the southern region of Mexico, Dr. Milton Leof, and his indefatigable collaborator, Daniel Brenmann. The overpowering creative drive of the Olmecs, emanating from Guerrero and so prolific in many other regions of Mesoamerica, will be clearly indicated in this book, which we hope will soon be published. It will also contain a reproduction of the eternal Semitic counterpart of the Olmecs, a wonderful stone sculpture in the Leof Collection. I consider this masterpiece by an unknown Mexcala artist to be one of the most impressive representations of a person of Semitic race.

Figures from Tlatilco (central plateau of Mexico), of the middle pre-Classic period, which clearly show the distinction between quite different racial types. The young girl and boy *(above)* may be regarded as representative of the white element (termed by me 'Contra-Olmecs'), whereas the figure *below, left* is purely Olmec and Asiatic in character. Height of upper figures 11 cm; of lower figures 16 cm and 9 cm. *Cf. pp. 94, 95.*

Heads from Tlatilco, dating from the middle pre-Classic, which likewise indicate distinctly the great ethnic diversity that existed at this time. Height of figure at top, centre 14.5 cm; of the small heads to the right and left 4 cm; all the others are about three-quarters of their actual size except that in the centre of the second row, which is 14 cm high. *Cf. p. 95.*

Heads from Tlapacoyan, dating from the middle pre-Classic. The head *above*, *left* represents the Asiatic element, and the other two in the top row the white element. Of great interest are the two actors (below), who are strongly suggestive of our court jesters. Height: above, from left to right: 7 cm, 11.5 cm, 3.5 cm; below 10 cm, 11 cm. *Cf. pp. 95, 96.*

Figurines from Tlapacoyan, likewise from the pre-Classic of the plateau of Mexico. *Above, left:* Olmec woman. Height 7.5 cm. *Above, right:* a very rare rendering, in which a man (left) and woman (right) are combined. Height 9.5 cm. The other types are very lively and true to nature. Height of head in centre 7 cm; of that below, left 10 cm; of figure below, right 14 cm. *Cf. p. 95.*

of Guerrero which have a great affinity with early Teotihuacán ware. Although we know how far many Teotihuacán objects travelled and that the sacred shrine had an almost inter-continental importance, it is strange that precisely in early, primitive times so many trade objects found their way to Guerrero or were copied there. Moreover, it might not be out of the question that certain early ceramic figurines from Guerrero which I shall call 'flat faces' PLATE P. 66 may have been forerunners of a stylistic tendency at Teotihuacán. To be sure, the idea of representing human faces on a flat plane and in horizontal equilibrium, such as were often produced in the south, PLATE P. 66 UPPER ROW reached a high point of artistic expression in the famous classical stone masks of Teotihuacán. The whole idea, however, contrasts very obviously with the decidedly vertical tendencies of pre-Classic figurines of the Pacific coast. Why and where this reversal of tendencies took place in the south is an enigma which probably can be explained only by positing a completely new shift of population units in that region. According to this theory the 'vertical' people, who were most likely already on the verge of degeneration, were absorbed or annihilated by the 'flat face' people. Be that as it may, a great deal of research work is still necessary to resolve these fundamental questions in a satisfactory manner.

II. THE CENTRAL PLATEAU

1. The Pre-Classic Period

The earliest epoch in the history of the central plateau of Mexico is still fairly obscure. The research work of George Vaillant and others mentioned previously has given us a fairly useful skeleton, revolving mainly around the localities of Zacatenco, Arbolillo, Tlatilco, Ticumán etc.; yet many things remain vague and unsolved. In addition, the new terracotta finds made during the last *Tlapacoyan finds* ten years at Tlapacoyan, a small village near Mexico City, have added to the many riddles of the plateau cultures. Tlapacoyan, in very early times an island at the eastern tip of the great lake of Tenochtitlán, was thus situated in the opposite direction from Tlatilco, with which it has many affinities but also some differences. Unfortunately up to now the haphazard finds in this eastern section of the Valley of Mexico have not been sufficiently evaluated and, even more disastrously, have often been destroyed by illegal digging and by the bulldozers of road-builders.

However, judging from the material available, I am inclined to *Olmecs* believe that Tlapacoyan witnessed the initial arrival of the Olmecs on the plateau of Mexico.

Geographically this seems logical, provided one accepts the premise that our strange, semi-Asiatic guests migrated from the south. They would thus have passed, over the lowest pass near Amecameca, from Morelos into the plateau valley, which otherwise was surrounded by formidable mountain ridges. But the newcomers found other people already established there, who quite obviously were of an entirely different stock and whose origin and provenance is still rather enigmatic. Lacking any definite denomination, I shall call *'Contra-Olmecs'* these people the 'Contra-Olmecs', because they developed side by side with the Olmecs (although they were present earlier), and later

94

mingled with them extensively. These people produced one of the most curious phenomena of pre-Columbian art history. Tlapacoyan pieces are more primitive, probably older, more robust and on the whole of much greater diversity than the Tlatilco ones which were presumably later, finer and more graceful. Whoever has had the good fortune to sit on top of the small mountain cone above Tlapacoyan, looking toward the snow-covered volcanoes in the east in the late afternoon, will never forget the impressive natural panorama which God has bestowed on that privileged site. Involuntarily one begins to muse and meditate, and suddenly one feels closer to the creative spirit of the ancient people who lived in this region. All at once one begins to comprehend why these people settled precisely at this spot, and why as far back as pre-Classic times the first square pyramid of Mesoamerica was built at this location.

PLATES PP. 89, 90, 91, 92, 105

In addition we should take note that at this spot there probably took place the first intensive racial mixture on the American continent. Witness thereof are the many artistic human representations of different varieties and intensities, rightly called by André Malraux 'the Voices of Silence'. They come from the soil of Tlapacoyan and Tlatilco and in the future might emerge from other places at present unknown to us. Quite obviously there existed at these locations types of human beings who in no way resembled Indians as they are known today and who were, in addition, diametrically opposed in aspect to the semi-Asiatic Olmecs. This is the reason I call these mysterious unknown people the 'Contra-Olmecs'. They had narrow faces, long curved noses and beards, and—in the case of the female figures—delicately cut profiles with fine straight noses (sometimes even turned slightly upwards). Their strongly modelled chins and on the whole their clearly defined physiognomical characteristics give us a very distinct idea of the living models for these ancient works of art. The slow merging of the native population was an inevitable process which can be studied very well at the Tlapacoyan site. In contrast, at Tlatilco usually the neatly defined Olmec type can be found representing the male and also the spiritually more active element (magicians, acrobats etc.). Most remarkable of all is the early appearance at both Tlatilco and Tlapa-

PLATE P. 92

PLATE P. 89

PLATES PP. 83, 90, 91

coyan of Negroid types shown in many photographs in this book.*
Another important offshoot or lateral branch of Olmec ceramics has
recently been found in Las Bocas (near Izúcar de Matamoros) in
the state of Puebla, typologically related to the style of Tlatilco and

PLATES PP. 106,
111

*Regression in late
pre-Classic*

Tlapacoyan. Further particulars will be given in the description of
District III (Puebla-Oaxaca).

During the epoch of the so-called late pre-Classic (a few hundred
years before the Christian era) a fundamental change seems to have
occurred in the whole central region of Mexico, which is distinctly
noticeable in the ceramics. Gone is the age of highly sophisticated
human representations and very stylized animal sculptures, as well
as the exquisite noble pottery. These are replaced by a rough and
much more primitive ware. Here we also have to consider the impact
of radical shifts of population as causing such a definite regression.

---

* The most beautiful Negro representations were made by the Mixtecs, and therefore are post-Classic
(see Plates on pages 113 and 181c). Besides this it is also interesting that the deity of the jewellers, Naualpilli,
mentioned in the Florentine Codex (IX.79 in the University of Utah edition, 1959), is still represented in
this late post-Classic era with kinky hair, which either might go back to very ancient Olmec traditions or to
influences from South America (see footnote 6 in chapter VII, page 160). R. G. Granados quotes the listing
in the register of Mexican antiquities of the Archivo de Indios of a green stone head which had kinky hair
made of gold and weighed (the Spaniards were very exact) 17 pesos and 4 tamines.

During the last International Congress of Americanists (1964) a French anthropologist said that the only
thing missing in connection with the Negroid terracottas of Ancient America were Negro skeletons, which
had still to be found and excavated. More than thirty years ago a German scholar, whom I personally
served as a cultural attaché in Buenos Aires, found Negro skulls in very deep layers in Argentina. Also in
Brazil Negro skeletons are said to have been found recently. I do not know if any have ever turned up in
Mesoamerica. Unless anyone searches for them, it is very unlikely that they will be discovered. Taking as a
base the terracotta ratio of, for instance, one to one thousand (1 : 1000), it would be very fortuitous indeed
to find accidentally the only Negro skull among so many others. However, it would be worth while, in my
opinion, to attempt a more serious investigation in this respect. To begin with, I would recommend the
region around Tres Zapotes in southern Veracruz!

At this point one might also refer to the research work recently conducted by Dr. Alfonso L. de Garay, who
claims to have found Negro characteristics in blood tests among the Lacandon Indians, one of the most
secluded Maya tribes of Mexico. The research has not been completely finished, but probably will soon be
published for the general public. Dr. de Garay is Director of the Genetic Program of the National Com-
mission for Nuclear Energy in Mexico.

Six further representations from the same culture as the twins reproduced on page 84, which have
the same primitive style but at the same time are very naturalistic. Note that the undeniable resemblance to early Japanese terracottas continues as late as this period. Height: *(a)* 20 cm; *(b)* 11 cm;
(c) 18 cm; *(d)* 18 cm; *(e)* 27 cm; *(f)* 22 cm.

The era of Ticumán (c. 500 BC) reveals products already of an inferior quality, and the ceramics excavated near the pyramid of Cuicuilco (buried by the eruption of the Xitli volcano, c. 300 BC) can hardly be compared to the highly sophisticated pottery of the preceding epochs. An exception to this development, however, are certain clay figurines which have appeared, usually during excavations for new buildings, under the lava crust of the Pedregal of San Angel, a suburb of Mexico City. Some very interesting objects were excavated here that are not easily dated. As the lava bed, which has various thicknesses, had the effect of 'sealing' the area, these objects all belong to the pre-Classic period; there are also many typological aspects which likewise prove their affinity with the categories of an early epoch.

PLATE P. 103

2. TEOTIHUACÁN OR CLASSIC PERIOD

After a certain interim period of an undetermined nature, which must have lasted for a few centuries immediately before and after the birth of Christ, a new cultural phenomenon appeared and made a grandiose start. This new factor, which was to overshadow all previous achievements, was the sacred city of Teotihuacán. What led to this phenomenon is still not sufficiently clear. It is difficult to determine from the evidence presently available whether survivors from Tlapacoyan had something to do with it, or whether (as I am inclined to believe) influences from Guerrero or from the Huasteca in the north were involved. Yet perhaps all these influences contributed in some way or other to the growth of this imposing cultural colossus. We should not forget that the Lake of Mexico, in the centre of the plateau, covered a much larger area 1700 years ago and extended as far as the neighbourhood of Teotihuacán. This enormous water basin, where fishing was surely carried on from

*Origins of
Teotihuacán*

A fine bearded head executed in Toltec style, said to have been found at Chiapas. A head with almost identical facial features, of the same size but depicted within the jaws of a snake, is housed in the Museo Diego Riviera, Anahuacalli, Mexico City. The head shown here does indeed suggest a portrait of the legendary figure of Quetzalcóatl. Note the cross motif on the forehead. Post-Classic. Actual size.

99

the earliest times, was quite naturally a central communication point between all the settlements that were established on its shores in the middle pre-Classic epoch. The catastrophic eruption of the Xitli volcano near Cuicuilco caused the destruction of vast tracts of land on the south side of the lake and undoubtedly forced large contingents of the population to emigrate. It is logical to believe that the refugees would have chosen the opposite shore of the lake for their new settlements. As a matter of fact, the earliest primitive ceramics of Teotihuacán I are quite similar to those found at Cuicuilco.

The untiring efforts of archaeologists and the reconstruction work undertaken by the Mexican government on the stupendous architectural remnants of Teotihuacán have brought to light a great deal of surprising material, especially with regard to the early Classic period. It is to be hoped, and can be expected, that heightened interest in the exploration of this unique cultural site will permit many more secrets to be extracted from the earth and will give fresh clues to assist us in understanding the development of this great 'mother culture' of Mesoamerica.

Painting and sculpture

It may be that the most important aspect of Teotihuacán lies in its concept of highly disciplined urban planning and its incomparable correlation of negative space and the positive volumes of the temple structures. Great significance may also be attached to the newly discovered fresco paintings, which surpass in quality those known previously. The sculpture produced at Teotihuacán during the various epochs was also of the same high artistic quality. Let us mention only the colossal hewn block called the Earth Goddess, which formerly stood in front of the Moon Pyramid, the dynamically protruding stone sculptures of the Quetzalcóatl Temple at the so-called 'Citadel', and last but not least the superb and uniquely classical stone masks used in burial rites. All phases of this sculptural development were accompanied in a worthy manner by the works of able ceramists, who knew how to interpret the human form. They had ample opportunity to observe the population, for huge crowds of residents of the city as well as pilgrims must have gathered for ceremonies at the great temples.

To begin with, let us mention the representations of dancers, which seem so lively. They were done with a quick, sketchy technique which expressed the essential movements in a very convincing manner by the simplest means. Among the ceramics are jointed dolls and all sort of figurines, which enable us to observe down to the last detail even the type of costume used in those days. An immense number of ornamental accessories for incense-burners represent a variety of deities, often shown with human features. Whole series of noble faces sculpted in clay (and which can now best be studied in the Diego Rivera Museum in Mexico City) compete in artistic perfection with beautiful stone masks used for the great funeral ceremonies of priestly chiefs. The ceramics were applied to incense-burners or used for offerings, in which case they were buried in the ground.

The so-called 'portrait heads' are a chapter unto themselves; they were manufactured by the mould technique in enormous quantities during the Classic period. In the 'group' picture shown on page 104 one can perceive which heads might have come from the same mould. Nevertheless a great margin of variety in the features is noticeable, because specialists in retouching procedures (not unlike those used by today's photographers) were busily at work correcting the individual heads before they were fired. Thus quite varied physiognomical effects were achieved. Yet the typical Teotihuacán type remains unmistakable. The only occasions when we encounter similar faces are in the early Classic Huasteca pieces and then later in Veracruz, where some influences of the mould-and-retouch technique can also be seen.

'Portrait heads'
PLATE P. 104

The world of classic forms of Teotihuacán is of an extraordinarily simple and harmonious beauty. Even in the small incense-burner accessories a wealth of pure forms can be seen that in its self-assured elegance has never been equalled again. The stylization of plants was masterfully achieved. Asymmetrical themes, such as a sheaf of feathers swung toward one side, were represented with natural grace. Everything the Teotihuacán artist touched, from the wonderful abstract treatment of the melting together of rectangle, triangle and circle to the simplified shell and flower motifs on an 'agriculture' temple, breathe the atmosphere of a pure, balanced and mature art. To be sure, also in Teotihuacán there came a period of decline in the quality of artistic products. The later works are overladen, the representations schematic and uninteresting as a consequence of endless repetition.

3. The Toltecs and Aztecs of the Post-Classic Period

Toltecs

In the tenth, eleventh and twelfth centuries the Toltecs succeeded the peoples of Teotihuacán. Their artistic achievements in architecture and sculpture remained on a remarkably high level, without attaining the outstanding greatness that characterized Teotihuacán. The more recent works are stiffer, more stylized and, one might say, even brutal and radical by comparison with Teotihuacán products. The excavations at Tula, the Toltec capital, testify to this. Toltec ceramics are less important than those of Teotihuacán, with the exception of some later Azcapotzalco products which must still be considered as belonging to the Toltec tradition.

Radiation of Toltec influence

The dominant influence of Toltec art on the architecture and sculpture of the post-Classic Maya region of the Yucatán peninsula is well known. It appeared after the great Toltec migration in the eleventh century. In many other parts of Mesoamerica one can detect ramifications of Toltec cultural influence without finding any examples of superior ceramics. At this point, however, I should like to mention a very curious piece of clay sculpture, which because of its special artistic merits has been included among the illustrations in this book and which has a vague connection with the Toltec world. The piece was found recently near the border of Michoacán

PLATE P. 84

and Guerrero. It represents two figures standing on the lid of a funerary urn. The whole atmosphere emanating from these twin figures, who seem to be singing or praying to higher spirits, invoking them to intercede for the deceased, render it a remarkable exponent of pre-Columbian ceramics. The intensity of its simplified abstraction makes it extremely interesting to compare it with our modern art. Here again we see the ability of the ancient artists of

Above: figurines discovered under the lava crust of the Pedregal. *Left:* part of a tripod or incense-burner. Height 8.5 cm. *Centre:* another figure reminiscent of archaic Japanese art. *Right:* female figure, typical of many pre-Classic renderings and suggestive of fertility cults. The figures in the middle and on the right are reproduced here in their actual size. *Below:* three figures of the early pre-Classic of Cuautitlán, plateau of Mexico. Height 11.5 cm. *Cf. p. 99.*

Heads from Teotihuacán illustrating the 'portrait' art of the Classic period. The small heads in the top row are depicted in their actual size; the group of twenty small heads *(inset, left)* are half their actual size. Height of heads on the right: centre 7 cm; below 2.5 cm. *Cf. p. 101.*

The large head *above, centre* originates from Puebla, those on the left and right from Tlatilco. The ➝ heads *below* are from Tlapacoyan. Middle pre-Classic. This style is widely disseminated. Height: above (from left to right): 10 cm, 18 cm, 11 cm; below 16 cm, 20 cm. *Cf. pp. 95, 108.*

Figures from the pre-Classic of Puebla. The female and male characteristics are very well brought out. Height of figure in the centre 23 cm; of that above, left 15.5 cm; above, right: profile view of this figure on the same scale; below, left 16 cm; below, right 18 cm. *Cf. p. 96.*

the New World, with their sensitive approach and extraordinary understanding of sculptural values.

As a whole, however, the ceramic output of the post-Classic period cannot be considered equal to that of former times, at least so far as the plateau of Mexico is concerned. This holds true especially for the last episode in pre-Columbian art, the Aztec period.

The lake city of Tenochtitlán, the capital of the Mexícas (now generally known as Aztecs), became the spiritual and political centre of a great empire. Like ancient Rome and many other metropolitan cities, Tenochtitlán must in its time have had a magnetic effect on all artists. Whether the influx of creative talent was always voluntary is an open question. Whereas the architecture with its concept of urban planning and formal development strictly adheres to the prototypes of Teotihuacán and Tula, the stone sculpture in the round rises to what may be called a culminating point in the post-Classic epoch as such. Its inherent monumental character is a unique achievement, permeated throughout by the most intense religious feeling, reflected even in the smallest works or, as might be said, miraculously present in its innermost core. Paul Westheim raises the question whether the 'Aztec' masterpieces may have been made by Totonacs for their Aztec overlords. Thus the works would have been executed by the heirs of the most illustrious stone sculptors of the Classic epoch. In any case, the artists must have been completely imbued with a fanatical religious spirit, expressed so strongly in these grandiose community masterpieces.

In Aztec ceramics we are able, however, to note a conspicuous retrogression, with the exception of some very fine pottery which displays Mixtec stylization tendencies and was made, we may be reasonably sure, by racial representatives of this Indian tribe. Aztec production proper was almost always from moulds and was usually dedicated to small figures of deities, which were *de rigueur* in every household at Tenochtitlán and in every Mexican settlement. These figures are the exact equivalent to the mass-produced 'holy pictures' of our day, which cannot usually be considered as a glorious chapter in the history of art.

Aztecs

III. PUEBLA AND OAXACA

Olmec influence

PLATE P. III

PLATE P. 105

Until recently very little of significance was known about ceramics in the extensive Puebla area. It was only when figures in a purely Olmec style were found in the neighbourhood of Izúcar de Matamoros (Las Bocas) that art connoisseurs and anthropologists began to become excited about the region. It had long been known that archaic pottery and figures were produced on a primitive level, with a relatively crude technique. On closer inspection it has now become apparent that at least the western part of Puebla must have had direct cultural links with the central plateau of Mexico. This is clearly indicated by the examples of terracottas shown here. The large head in the centre is from Puebla and demonstrates the artist's thorough command of a highly developed ceramic technique. The expressive face with the little snub nose and the interesting headdress make it another example of what may be called the 'Contra-Olmec' racial type. Below are seen, in reduced scale, two heads found at Tlapacoyan. Both the bearded man, the prototype of many later representations, and the woman (on the left) suggest an admixture of Asiatic blood. The two small figures above come from Tlatilco. Both these enchanting girls are again excellent examples of 'Contra-Olmecs' of the middle pre-Classic period.

Female figurines

PLATE P. 106

Further evidence in favour of the theory that white people were on American soil in archaic times is afforded by the rather primitive female sculptures from Puebla which depict the body in a quite exuberant, Rubens-like manner. The full-bearded man with the loin-cloth and the 'smart' cap is also a specimen indicating the presence of white blood. Another such example is the charming nude in the centre of the photograph, a masterpiece of artistic maturity in representation of the female form. This girl and the others shown above belie the assertion that in pre-Columbian times no artists existed who could express the beauty of the human body. To be sure, no great female statues were produced in America, but womanly women and girlish girls were thoroughly appreciated and very well represented!

The figurines recently found in the Puebla region are achievements PLATE P. 111 of extremely fine merit. The maturity of the artistic concept in these pieces would be a surprising revelation to many connoisseurs of art. With admirable ease and a very exact purpose, the artist has represented the human form using the directness of an almost insolently primitive technique. And yet the total artistic concept is preserved and beautifully presented. We are confronted with a unique and final solution, with a total sculptural experience.

To the south-east of Puebla lies the region of the Zapotecs and Mixtecs, famous for its two sacred shrines, Monte Albán and Mitla, near the present city of Oaxaca. Particularly the older site, Monte Albán, which has been thoroughly investigated by archaeologists, gives the visitor an excellent insight into the fascinating and imposing world at an ancient temple district. For millennia this site served as the scene for the celebration of solemn religious rites.

Here, as nearly everywhere else in Mexico, Olmec influence was in evidence at the beginning of cultural development. This is convincingly demonstrated by the famous reliefs of the 'Dancers' from the first building period. I would assume that again the original PLATE P. 110 nucleus from which this culture originated has to be looked for in Guerrero. The unusual thing about the archaic reliefs is that these voluminous figures, although primitive, are definitely shown in motion, whereas normally very early works of art are static and immobile. It may at first seem strange that in Guerrero we should find miniature figures of ancient provenance which emphasize precisely this element of movement. An example from Altamirano in the region of the lower Balsas River, a stream which certainly served as a gateway for many migrations, is shown in our plate. PLATE P. 112

In the vicinity of Monte Albán the subsoil is teeming with *tepalcates* (clay sherds). So far as pre-Classic figures are concerned no outstanding works have been discovered, but there are always exceptions to the rule. I have seen some remarkable pieces from the region of Etla (north-east of Monte Albán) in a private collection in Oaxaca, and again I must underscore the more or less strong

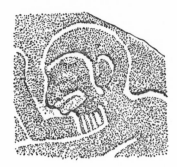

FIGS. 8, 9 – *Left: head of a dancer. Olmec type; pre-Classic. Stone relief, Monte Albán I, Oaxaca. Right: head of a dancer. Semitic type, the eternal antagonist of the Olmecs; pre-Classic. Stone relief, Monte Albán I, Oaxaca.*

Olmecoid influence in Monte Albán I, which shows a certain affinity with Guerrero pieces.

Sculptures at Monte Albán

However, some extraordinarily subtle clay sculptures have been found from the early Classic epoch at Monte Albán. Among these are the impressive 'grave guardians' published in Linné's volume on *Ancient America* in the ART OF THE WORLD series, whose 'warding-off' gestures will be remembered by anyone who has seen them. Although the Zapotecs were assiduous ceramists, as is proven by the great number of funerary urns to be seen in collections, the purely human side of the picture is usually secondary. The overpowering world of the deities seems to have blacked out everything else. The Olmec influence also seems to have disappeared completely. Its place was taken by the pure Indian, here clearer discernible at an early date. (Witnesses thereof are the noble faces of gods and goddesses of Monte Albán II.) To this epoch also belongs the famous priestly urn in the National Museum of Anthropology in Mexico City, which shows a very princely type of human being.

PLATE P. 112

Two more examples are also good illustrations of this type. On the lower right is a clean-cut profile of a man of very noble racial extraction, on the left a small urn with a female head. Here also we notice the double concept so often discernible in pre-Columbian art; on one hand the stress on powerful, energetic and manly features,

Olmec masterpieces from Las Bocas, Puebla. Height: above 12 cm; below 8.5 cm. *Cf. pp. 96, 108.*

Above, centre: large portrait head with fresco painting, from the so-called 'Mixtequilla', an area of southern Veracruz which had some kind of connection with the Mixtecs. Post-Classic. Height 25 cm. *Above, left and right:* miniature of an Olmec dancer, from Altamirano, Guerrero. Actual size. *Below:* Zapotec terracottas from the Oaxaca area. Classic. Height of figure on the left 18 cm; of that on the right 11 cm. *Cf. pp. 109, 110.*

Large Negroid head. Mixtec, from Oaxaca. Post-Classic. Height 18 cm. Josué Saenz Collection, Mexico City. *Below, right:* small Mixtec head. Post-Classic. Height 13 cm. Preussischer Kulturbesitz, Staatliche Museen, Berlin. *Cf. pp. 113, 115.*

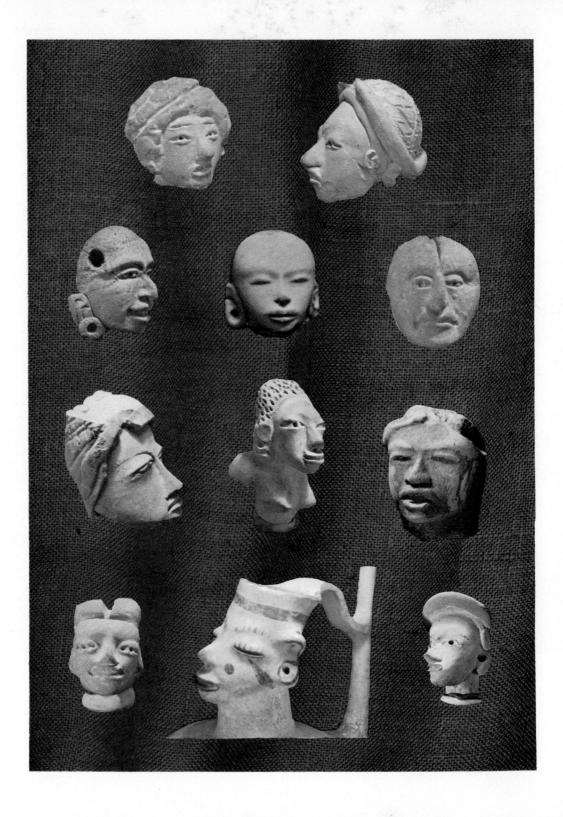

and on the other an emphasis on the charmingly natural, feminine aspect, both apparent only when no mysterious 'gods' are present. The cultural heirs of the Zapotecs were the Mixtecs. They are well known for their extraordinarily fine craftsmanship in jewellery of all kinds, a collection of which is one of the great treats of the Monte Albán Museum in the city of Oaxaca.

Mixtecs

The Mixtecs belong to the post-Classic period and were surely in contact with the Toltecs, as Linné rightly observed. An especially elegant head of a chieftain is reproduced in the centre of our plate. It most certainly comes from the 'Mixtequilla' region in southern Veracruz, which borders on Mixtec territory. This beautiful piece still has touches of colour done in a fresco technique and undoubtedly belongs to the post-Classic period. The Mixtecs continued their original line of development until they were the unrivalled leaders in the field of ceramics prior to the Spanish conquest. A wonderful example of their brilliant technical ability, their understanding of form and colour, and their prolific ideas in design and composition has already been shown in the colour plate on page 29. The picture on this simple object reminds one in an almost 'spooky' manner of a modern painting of very good quality.

PLATE P. 112

PLATE P. 29

To illustrate the Mixtecs' capacity to represent human beings we may refer to three heads. The large one on page 113 is a ceramic masterpiece, both in technical execution and in artistic concept. The surprising thing about this piece is that it hardly suggests an 'accidental' stylization made by an Indian. How the appearance of Negro elements came about in this late post-Classic period is still a riddle. The smaller female head is an important piece from the Berlin-Dahlem Museum and also shows slightly Negroid features.

PLATE P. 113

PLATE P. 113

Collection of portrait heads from Huasteca, showing a large variety of different racial types. All of them are pre-Classic or early Classic except the figure in the middle of the bottom row, which is post-Classic and may have served as a decoration on a so-called 'tea-pot', such as was common in Huasteca. From various private collections in New York and Mexico City. Height: above, left 5 cm; above, right 6 cm; second row, all figures 4.5 cm; third row, from left to right, 7 cm, 6 cm, 8 cm; bottom row 5.5 cm, 7 cm, 7 cm. *Cf. p. 122.*

PLATE P. 181 A third specimen of this type, which belongs to the National Museum of Anthropology in Mexico City, is shown on page 181 (lower left). In this figure – there is no point in quibbling – a real Negro is represented, in this case very true to nature indeed. Only recently I 'discovered' this rare and hitherto disregarded figure in the superbly organized storerooms of the new National Museum of Anthropology in Mexico City.

Page 117: Huasteca figures. *(a)*: mother and child, the mother with typical distended body. Pre-Classic. Height 22 cm. *(b)*: seated girl, likewise pre-Classic. Height 12 cm. *(c)*: pretty figure of a pregnant woman. Classic period. The face is mould-cast. Height 14 cm. *Cf. p. 122.*

Page 118: Development of the representation of the human figure in Veracruz. *(a)*, *(c)*: early Remojadas figures. Pre-Classic. Height 12.5 cm. *(b)*: amusing jester figure which to us suggests a puppet. Height 17 cm. *(d)*: Classic (Indian-Oriental) head of sun priest with Olmec mouth and filed or mutilated teeth. Height 23 cm. *(e)*: small head with stuck-on beard and snake motif on forehead. Height 9 cm. *(f)*: a thoroughly Negroid representation. Height about 9 cm. *Cf. pp. 131, 138.*

Page 119: One of the most impressive clay sculptures in pre-Columbian art. Late pre-Classic period of Veracruz. *Cf. p. 132.*

a

b

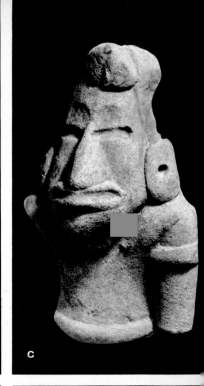

c

d

e

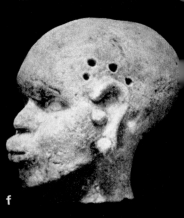

f

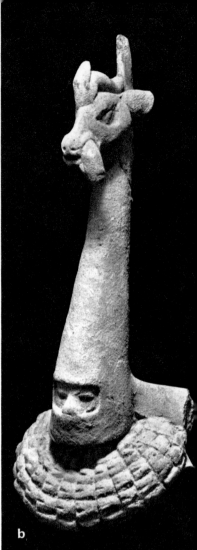

a

b

c

IV. THE EAST: THE GULF COAST
AND THE HINTERLAND

From the point of view of archaeology and art history, all the ancient cultures which developed on the shores of the Gulf of Mexico and in the hinterland of each of these districts are usually combined in one large region known as the eastern cultures (IV). As has already been mentioned, this extensive region extends from the lower reaches of the Panuco River (near the port of Tampico) in the north to the state of Tabasco in the south. It has three areas with greatly differentiated types of art. All three of them, however, were inhabited already in pre-Classic times and were active centres of early cultures. Whereas in the extreme south the sources of art slowly dried up, the contrary is true in the northern regions. Particularly in the central part of Veracruz, a steady evolution led to a superb climax of artistic accomplishment in clay sculpture.

1. THE HUASTECA

A glance at the map enables one to see that the Panuco River could serve equally well as a gateway from the east or Atlantic side of Mexico as the Balsas River did on the southern or Pacific side. The Panuco River was indeed used in this way by those people whom we now call the Huastecans. Who the earliest settlers really were is not known. To judge by their language, they were related to the Mayas who settled to the south. Perhaps they were separated from this group in the middle pre-Classic period by an Olmec wedge, which

Earliest settlers

(a): female dancer, her arms outstretched and the upper part of her body naked, wearing a realistically rendered ornamental skirt and imaginative head-dress. Height 38 cm. (b): theatrical head-dress of a 'doe dancer' (fragment). The game has been killed (as is visible from the lolling tongue). Height 18 cm. (c): dancer, of the purest Indian racial stock, shown in profile; the sharpness of the features is superb. Height 9 cm. Fragment, from the private collection of Señor Ricardo Hecht. (a) is early Classic, (b) middle Classic, and (c) late Classic; all are from Veracruz. Cf. p. 137.

can be traced from Tres Zapotes in southern Veracruz south to La Venta in Tabasco. Not long ago we knew almost nothing about the art of these mysterious people, who in historical times were considered by the Aztecs to be barbarians. The only evidence we had of their culture were two stone figures in the National Museum of Anthropology in Mexico City, but the famous richly tattooed male statue known as 'the Adolescent' very definitely vouched for their great artistic talent, in spite of the popular Aztec opinion. The aggressive Aztec master race reacted strongly against the art of other civilizations (as did the Greeks), particularly when religious and moral principles were involved. And the Huastecans always remained independent of the cultural zone dominated by the inhabitants of Tenochtitlán. Considering the high level of Huastecan stone sculpture, it is no surprise that in more recent times ceramic PLATES PP. 114, 117 figures of great beauty have appeared, such as those shown on pages 114 and 117.

Figures In the earliest period there were produced some remarkable, unique figures with stylized long bodies and small heads. A charming conception is evident in the figure of a woman with a child peering around his mother's arm. The pre-Classic figurine on the upper right is a refined, simple and girlish piece which yet has a primitive touch. Simple and touching in its expressive power is the figure of the young pregnant woman on the lower right. Her slightly haggard face and the arms hanging listlessly by the budding womb point naturally and gracefully to her condition as an expectant mother.

Portrait heads
PLATE P. 114 With the collection of Huastecan portrait heads we begin a very interesting chapter in the early ethnological history of the Americas. Here, as on the plateau of Mexico and everywhere else in Mesoamerica, we find totally different racial types. The white element is predominant, and two faces with Semitic characteristics are also shown. Even Negroid features appear. The small classic female head (second row, centre), which reminds one of the best miniature portrait heads from Teotihuacán, and the beautifully modelled Negro woman (third row, centre) with delicate 'African' breasts, are masterpieces. The ceramic substance is a very light clay, typical of the Huasteca, which sometimes almost acquires the effect of fine

'biscuit' porcelain. It is remarkable that Asiatic influence is usually absent in this region. In the centre of the bottom row we see the head of a so-called Huastecan 'tea-pot' (a term invented by archaeologists), which already belongs to the post-Classic period. The woman's expression and make-up are so sophisticated, and the head so well integrated into the bulging upper portion of the vessel, that one can speak with assurance of its creator as a genius.

2. TABASCO AND LA VENTA

La Venta is situated in Tabasco, in the southernmost part of the *Principal sites* eastern region. It has acquired great fame because of its colossal Olmec stone heads and the establishment at this site of the first large, well-organized religious and architectural centre in the Americas. At this point any insistence on its importance is certainly superfluous.

Equally interesting are the Olmecan finds in Tres Zapotes and San Lorenzo, both in the southern region of the state of Veracruz. Most striking are the enormous Negro sculptures of the former site and the incredibly beautiful and powerful heads of the latter. The peculiar jadeite treasure cache, discovered by Matthew Stirling at La Venta, has been beautifully reproduced in colour in the new Skira book on pre-Columbian art. For us this discovery of a group of figurines is of special interest, since the entire ensemble was found in its original position—that is to say, with many highly polished small jadeite figures grouped around a single figure of totally different material, a reddish stone (possibly indicating an older terracotta piece). The background is formed by a row of elongated well-polished jadeite stones, in the arrangement of a palisade. At La Venta such stone palisades were erected to delimit what was probably the most sacred precinct. At this point I should like to mention the presence of a primitive stone palisade which I saw on a slope in the 'Ciudad Perdida' (also known as La Sabana) near Acapulco, the edges of which were marked with a series of dots. Unfortunately these markers and also a stone with a petroglyph of a fish from the same region are reported to have disappeared. Again and again one can notice certain clues that indicate the possibility of early Olmec penetration into the southern part of Guerrero.

Evolution of figures

In this book we have already seen many Olmec ceramic pieces which enable us to re-create the route which these artists probably took.

PLATE P. 143 In the plate on page 143 showing six La Venta pieces, I have attempted to demonstrate graphically the evolution of human representations of the Olmec type. We might consider the head in the centre of the top row as a truly aboriginal specimen. It comes from the important Feuchtwanger Collection in Mexico City. How strange it is to be confronted with such a realistic figure of a primitive man! Directly below, in contrast, is the figure of a woman, rare in Olmec art but when found usually of high artistic quality. The evocative PLATE P. 143 gesture of the raised hand arranging the hair, the slender and enchantingly feminine body, and the fine modelling of the arm prove once again how important a little bit of clay can be in developing our understanding of the sequences of art history. The piece on the right in the lower row is more formal, and one cannot deny its affinity with the large La Venta heads. On the whole we are accustomed to seeing Olmecs only in definitely and highly stylized versions. However, on the left and right in the top row are highly realistic representations which give us an excellent idea what two Olmecs actually looked like.

Finally, the illustrations include (lower row left) a beautifully pol-

Page 125: Veracruz head, showing a Negroid strain. Classic period. This is very clearly a work of portraiture. Height 17 cm. *Cf. p. 141.*

Page 126: *Left:* flautist. A superb and dramatic clay sculpture from the Josué Saenz Collection in Mexico City. It is a highly stylized Jalisco figure with deliberately exaggerated verticality. Classic. *Right:* two more archaic Nayarit figures of men, obviously likewise of Semitic origin, here characterized with great simplicity and spontaneous charm. The naturalistic treatment of these two figures and their inner contentment dispose of the false idea that they are caricatures. Height of detail on the left 25 cm; of Nayarit figures 16 cm. *Cf. p. 146.*

Page 127: The 'White Lady' of Jalisco. Classic. Probably one of the best female representations of Jalisco, directly related to the male figure reproduced in colour on p. 158. Height of detail about 30 cm. Private collection of Señora Raquel F. de Girault. *Cf. p. 147.*

a

b

c

d

FIGS. 10–12 *(left to right)*: 10 – *Olmec head with Negroid strain. Stone. Tuxtla.* 11 – *Semitic head. Stone. From Santa Lucía, Cozamaluapan, Guatemala.* 12 – *Clay sculpture of a Semitic head, from La Venta.*

FIG. 13 – *Negroid stone sculpture from Tres Zapotes.*

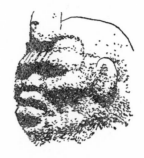

ished fragment from La Venta depicting with undeniable clearness a Negroid woman. Her presence should not seem strange if we take into consideration the strong Negroid traits obviously present in the monumental Olmec stone heads.

On the whole, our knowledge of the development and chronology of Olmec art as such and of its human representations is of relatively recent date. Just how new our understanding of this culture is can be demonstrated by the fact that such an eminent scholar, connoisseur and specialist as Walter Lehmann could write, in his *Alt-Mexikanische Kunstgeschichte*,* below the illustration of a terracotta fragment in unmistakable Olmec style: 'Olmec, probably already with Spanish influence'. On the other hand we may ascribe to the far-seeing intuition of Walter Lehmann and his unerring perception

* Published by Wasmuth in Berlin, 1921.

Figures from ancient Colima. *(a)*: standing figure executed in the so-called Archaic style, related to the figure reproduced on p. 158 (above, right). Height about 15 cm. *(b)*: pregnant woman with two children. Height about 17 cm. *(c)*: seated figure. It is suggestive of modern art, in that the mother's limbs are posed dramatically and the (sick?) child dangles from her back. Height about 12 cm. *(d)*: squatting man. Height about 14 cm. *Cf. p. 153.*

FIG. 14 – *Stone relief from La Venta (stele no. 3)*.

of their significance the fact that he juxtaposes on the same page two of the great counterparts in the art of ancient America: an Olmec head with Negroid traits from Tuxtla and a Semitic head, also of stone, from Santa Lucía, Cozamoluapan, Guatemala. We may assume this was done intentionally, as an allusion to the strong reciprocal tension between the most important types of personage in ancient American history, and which now on closer inspection is beginning to emerge more clearly. The Spanish art historian, J. Pijoán, who wrote a highly significant book on pre-Columbian art (*Summa Artis*, vol. X, Madrid, 1946), evidently had the same 'hunch'. Twenty-five years after Lehmann he demonstrated the same contrast in an excellent way by combining a Semitic-looking terracotta head from La Venta with the most Negroid of all pre-Columbian stone sculptures, a figure from Tres Zapotes now in Santiago Tuxtla, Veracruz.

In the footnote on page 88 I mentioned the continuously recurring duality between the two leading races, so very different, which incidentally can also be noticed in South America, in the gold collection of the Bank of Colombia in Bogotá. This matter will be discussed in chapter VII. Another convincing piece of evidence FIG. 14 relating to this question is the huge stone relief from La Venta (stele no. 3, measuring two and a half metres in height), now in the park of the museum at Villahermosa, Tabasco. The central and dominating figure of this relief was formerly called 'Uncle Sam' in an allusion to the United States. In reality we should attach to this unique monument a different historical meaning, which deserves to be considered carefully. In view of the knowledge recently acquired, it is not possible simply to ignore a piece of historical evidence of such large dimensions. The bold and energetic figure confronting us in such a realistic lively manner, radiating an almost cosmic intelligence, undoubtedly represents a prominent member of the Semitic group of people who once trod upon the ancient American stage.

3. Veracruz

The central part of the eastern cultural district, almost completely taken up by the present state of Veracruz, occupies a very special position in the history of terracotta art in the New World. Throughout all the various epochs of pre-Columbian times, unknown but greatly talented artists created fine clay sculptures in this region. The materials are extremely varied and the examples are numerous; therefore a few chronological and stylistic clues may be adduced here to bring some order into the matter. The oldest pre-Classic period is usually known under the collective name of 'Remojadas', *Earliest figures* derived from a site relatively near the city of Veracruz which is PLATE P. 118 especially abundant in early pieces. Some of the figures reproduced on page 118 illustrate this style. They show great similarity to many other pre-Classic pieces yet are easily recognizable because of a certain dignified concept, characteristic of most Veracruz clay sculptures. The two men (top row, left and right) once again suggest white and Semitic types. Several very interesting pictures reproduced in this book belong to the next, late pre-Classic group, which probably had certain connections with Remojadas but also bears great similarities to Huastecan art. This period is very well illustrated by the two heads reproduced on page 19 (bottom row, right and PLATE P. 19 left). Both are remarkable examples of the ceramics of the eastern district. The eye technique of the left figure seems strange, yet the general effect of the well-modelled face is not marred by it. The piece on the right is one of the most powerful Semitic representations I know of, almost comparable in its expressive force to the work of an artist such as Kaethe Kollwitz.

PLATE P. 119 So far as the early portrait character of the Veracruz school is concerned, the plate on page 119 (actual size) is of tremendous importance. It shows clearly the temperament of a powerful personage of those times. Observing the piece more carefully, one can hardly avoid being impressed by the compact, balanced and self-reliant will of this man. The bold profile, the almost brutally protruding, bearded jaw and the penetrating look are enough to startle any sensitive observer. A great American personality of remarkable strength has here been preserved for posterity in the humble material of clay.

Classic period In the ensuing Classic period we come to a quite different group, of dancers and more finely modelled figurines. A delight in movement and expressive dramatization, using a variety of forms, seems to have been imbedded in the consciousness of the artists of Mesoamerica. The history of community and group dancing of a sacred or worldly character is as old as the history of America itself. It began three thousand years ago in Tlatilco and is still very much alive, as is evident from the many dances performed at fiestas and in conjuction with Catholic ceremonies throughout Latin America.

Page 133: *(a)*, *(b)*: highly stylized Negroid heads, with many tattooing scars. From the early Classic period of Veracruz. Height: *(a)* 13 cm; *(b)*, *(c)* 17 cm. *(c)*: late Classic head of dancer with lavish head-dress. Height about 19 cm. *(d)*: early Semitic type. Height about 15 cm. *(b)* and *(c)* are from the Tulane University Collection, New Orleans, the other two from a private collection in Mexico City. *Cf. p. 138.*

Page 134: Fine Classic portrait heads from Veracruz. *(a)*: imposing bearded Negroid personage. Height about 21 cm. *(b)*: figure of a sage priest, typically introspective. Height about 19 cm. *(c)*: dancer in ecstasy, rendered by a towering snake mask. Height about 21 cm. *(d)*: powerful Indian ruler. Height about 19 cm. *(a)* is from a private collection in New York, *(b)* and *(d)* from the Kurt Stavenhagen Collection, and *(c)* from the Josué Saenz Collection, Mexico City. *Cf. p. 139.*

Page 135: Four masterly renderings of different human types, from Veracruz. Classic. *Above:* the two heads *(a)* and *(b)* belong to the category of 'smiling faces' (a unique feature of Totonac female dancers). Height: *(a)* 17 cm; *(b)* 15 cm. Private collection of Señora de Villafranca, Mexico City. *(c)*, *(d)* are likewise ethnic counterparts. Height: 18 cm, about 13 cm. *(c)* is from the Kurt Stavenhagen Collection, *(d)* from the Hankins Collection, Mexico City. *Cf. p. 139.*

a

b

c

d

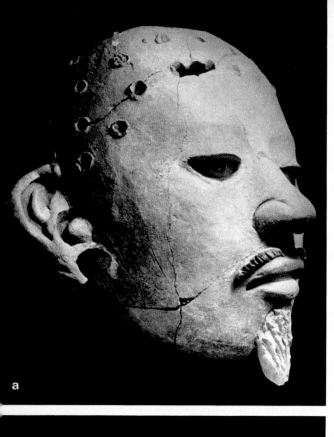

a

b

c

d

b

d

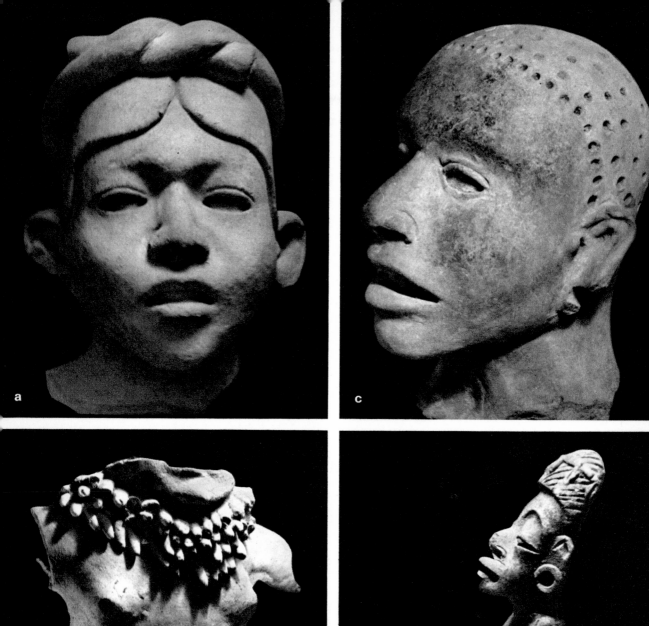

a

b

c

d

The figures shown on page 144 come from the region of Huachin, Veracruz. They represent a transitional style between the famous dancer terracottas of Teotihuacán and those made in the late Classic era of the Maya on the island of Jaina. The Teotihuacán pieces still preserve a rather primitive flavour on account of their obviously stuck-on heads. The Jaina ones, although beautiful, are already somewhat over-realistic and almost too theatrical in their sophisticated refinement. The ones shown here seem to represent an intermediate style. They are more gracious than the former, more vigorous than the latter. The rich costume of the corn dancer (recognizable by the corncobs attached to the head-dress), who carries a shield bearing a Maya design, is remarkable and could be copied to make an effective stage costume in our day. The figure on the left attracts our attention by the strikingly rendered position of the legs, the outstretched arms, and the concentrated expression on the face. It is difficult to captivate the whole artful movement in one photograph. The two heads in the bottom row, also from Huachin, are interesting in so far as the one on the right readily proves the connection between the Veracruz region and classical Maya culture, while the one on the left gives the peculiar impression of a realistic Tartar face with all its characteristic details. Typical of Veracruz is the large dancer making pantomime gestures shown on page 120; here again the features are not those of an Indian woman but are more like those of a Frenchwoman from Brittany! The pointed head-dress is reminiscent of Phoenician or Javanese fashions. The dramatic 'deer dancer 'on the right seems more akin to African models, and such a mask is still worn in ritual dances in Guinea. The more we search and the more that is found, the more

Transitional figures from Huachin

PLATE P. 120

Above (a), (c): the two finest Classic Veracruz heads in the State Museum in Jalapa, Veracruz. They are the embodiment of a fine Indian type, still found even today, when it was at the peak of its development. The girl is rendered in a movingly human and naturalistic manner. The extremely noble male head is related to the Berlin figure reproduced in colour on p. 149 and in black-and-white on p. 125. Height about 17 cm. *Below, left (b):* torso of a young Totonac female dancer. Classic. Height 21 cm. Collection of the author. *Below, right (d):* a superb rendering of a human body with Negroid characteristics. Likewise from the Classic period. Height about 17 cm. Kurt Stavenhagen Collection. *Cf. p. 140.*

137

varied, astounding and interesting the image of the pre-hispanic New World becomes.

Other Classic pieces The entire Classic period of Veracruz is so rich in beautiful human representations that one is at a loss to effect an appropriate selection for a book such as this. Yet I should like to make as extensive a presentation as possible to give the reader an approximate idea of the quality and amazing variety of artistic production in this area of PLATE P. 118 Mexico. Already on page 118 we met a great variety of human beings: a figure with a false beard in Egyptian style, which to complete the picture has a snake-like protrusion (unfortunately slightly mutilated) on the forehead. Below to the right is a perfect example of a Negress and in the top row (right and left) are two Semitic heads—the racial mixture helped to avoid boredom! A Mongoloid type, probably a priest of the sun, makes his appearance on the left side (bottom row). He also belongs to the Classic Totonac period, although his mouth with filed teeth is reminiscent of earlier Olmecan stylistic traditions. Finally, in the centre of the top row, we are presented with the town joker, a kin of 'Kasperl' (Punch), who ought not to be missing if we want a complete picture of the life of those times. This page alone seems to justify the motto from Goethe chosen for this book.

PLATE P. 133 The same can be said about page 133. Above are two vigorous Negro personalities, whose faces show particularly clear scarification tattooing, for which (as is well known) the Negro skin is especially suited. The origin of this custom as well as the general usage of earrings most likely has to be looked for in Africa. The first head on the left might also give the impression of an Asiatic earth demon, although the artist's interpretation seems quite human. On the lower right again is the Semitic representative, who never seems to be forgotten. It is only on the left side that we can finally admire a real Indian (late Classic) who boasts an especially elaborate head-dress. This handsome piece and the tattooed one on the upper right belong to the superb collection of pre-Columbian art at Tulane University in New Orleans. I am indebted to Professor Donald Robertson for his gracious help in taking these pictures during my delightful stay at Tulane in 1963.

The colour plate on page 149 is useful for an understanding of the *Portraiture in Veracruz*
art of portraiture in Veracruz. The splendid head in the upper row
on the left looks quite Negroid, and is studded with small holes on PLATE P. 149
the scalp, reminding one of the use of the same technique in Ife and
Benin sculptures. This beautiful piece is in the Museum für Völkerkunde, Berlin (Dahlem) and was purchased, probably more than
seventy years ago, by Walter Lehmann from Señor Batres, then
Director of the archaeological museum in Mexico City. According
to Lehmann the holes were used to attach hair or wool to the head.
The next head is one of the most noble creations of Veracruz. It
belongs, with the equally beautiful head on page 151, to the famous PLATE P. 151
Stavenhagen Collection in Mexico City. In the same collection is
also found the Negroid figure of a dancer (lower left), showing the
well-preserved ritualistic painting on her face. On the opposite side
is her more Mongoloid companion, with identical make-up.

Three pages of black-and-white illustrations complete the picture.
The first one also shows a Negroid head dotted with holes. Even if PLATE P. 134
this piece were the only one preserved from pre-hispanic times, the
fairy tale that the art of portraiture did not exist in pre-Columbian
art would collapse. One can hardly imagine a better depiction of a
human personality than this life-sized ceramic. The following head
gives a classical and realistic impression, reminding us very strongly
of well-known representations of Egyptian officials. On the right
side (bottom row) we finally perceive the noble and powerful
physiognomy of an Indian. The revealing and penetrating look of
the subject was superbly achieved by the application of a dot of tar
paint (*chapopote*) in the eyes, a method which was often used by the
Veracruz artist. Next to it we can spot a very unusual piece representing a dancer or priest wearing a mask over his head that is
crowned by two snakes. In the photograph only the chin of the
bearer of the mask can be seen, but his features are completely
modelled underneath his dramatic headgear.

In the next illustration we again see a startling mixture of racial PLATE P. 135
types. On the right (top row) is a lovely representation of one of the
most famous Veracruz styles, generally known under the name of
'smiling faces'. They are nearly always made in a mould and some- *'Smiling faces'*

139

times appear stereotyped. This specimen, however, has an individu-
alistic expression that gives us an excellent idea of what at least one
of these smiling people actually looked like. Net to this piece is an
extremely rare head in the same style, but with a strong Negroid
touch, proving that among these cheerful dancers there must have
been some of dark racial extraction. A peculiar mixture of Japanese
and Negroid elements is shown in the head on the lower left, which
also boasts a daring coiffure. Next to it, in complete contrast, is a
fully bearded white man.

Indian heads

PLATE P. 136

After all these strange figures, the real Indians finally come into
their own on page 136. The two heads in the top row, one female
and the other male, may be considered to represent the acme in
pre-Columbian art of portraiture. They belong to the magnificent
collection of the State Museum at Jalapa, Veracruz. On the lower
left is the simple but very sensitively modelled torso of a Totonac
girl. A highly sophisticated contrast is achieved by placing the
luxuriously extravagant necklace on the youthful, nude body. Next
to it appears a seated woman, who again seems to come from the
African continent rather than the American. Her poise, the structure
of her limbs, as well as all the details of the body are definitely those
of a Negress.

Finally we should mention eight masterpieces of Veracruz art which
we might select as comprising the most beautiful human representations in pre-Columbian ceramics. Three examples have already
been shown in the chapter dealing with the essential artistic values.

FRONT OF
SLIP-CASE

PLATE P. 60

One is the enchanting young woman reproduced on the slip-case
of this volume. She embodies the natural and unaffected approach
of the joyful, free, peaceful and creative people of Veracruz. It is
difficult to know what to admire first: the elegant and graceful
draping of the head-cloth, smartly polished with black tar paint,
the original movement of the arms and the hand, so well interpreted
from real life, the enticing twist of the young body with its small
breasts, or just the coquettish bow around the neck. Everything
combines to form a small but fascinating masterpiece. The two
other sculptures testify to the advanced state of a pure art of por-

PLATES PP. 45, 46

traiture. The first one, wearing a head-dress similar to an African

140

burnoose, is undoubtedly related to the fine head in the Berlin Museum (page 149). On the face, the same expression can be noticed, possibly softer and more genial but in any case an expression often peculiar to the psychic disposition of certain Negroid people. The second head, also of almost natural size, is surely of as fine a quality as any achievement in the world of art. The work is of serious content since it obviously depicts a dead person. It gives one the feeling that the deceased was beloved and therefore is being mourned, his portrait conceived and executed in a mood of reverent affection.

Another definitely portrait-like representation is the Negroid face shown on page 125. Although a little rougher is execution, the work conveys a very strong and true-to-life expression. In the colour plate on page 150 we see two relatively small heads (10 centimetres high); on the left is a warrior wearing a casque and on the right a priest with a tall head-dress, symbolizing his high rank, which almost (like a papal tiara) seems to crush the diminutive face. The warrior radiates something incredibly human and uncommonly attractive. His friendly face captivates us and excites our brotherly sympathy. The priest, on the other hand, although also extremely human, is a great introspective and spiritual personality of a most aristocratic sort. The fine nose, the half-closed eyes and above all the slight touch of mockery and scorn around his sensitive mouth heighten the impression of a man of exceptional intelligence and spirituality. He must have inspired great esteem, reverence and admiration among his contemporaries. The two remaining heads on page 150 represent an adolescent and a woman, who should be understandable enough even to art critics who are accustomed to seeing only European works of art. The same holds true for the large head in the Stavenhagen Collection shown in the colour plate on page 151. Every single one of the eight exceptionally fine pieces just discussed embodies in its own way the dignity and self-reliant gracefulness of the early inhabitants of America.

PLATE P. 45

PLATE P. 46

PLATE P. 125

PLATE P. 150

PLATE P. 150

PLATE P. 151

V. THE WEST

In the pre-Columbian world the western section, that is to say District V on our map, extends from Nayarit to Michoacán. Its art differs fundamentally from that of the rest of Mesoamerica. In the west we do not find vast temple cities planned on an enormous scale, huge stone monuments, or choice jewellery of gold and precious stones. Instead we find an abundance of wonderful, original and indeed unique ceramics. The whole creative energy of the western people seems to have been concentrated on this special field of artistic activity. They invented, renewed and produced ceramics in substantial quantities, always with a great deal of variety. All the weight of their industry was placed on the production of images of plain human beings. They made neither gods nor single personages (the grand portrait), nor even static types of a less than individual stamp, such as we are accustomed to see in other regions. These western people were, however, well acquainted with various experiences of life and with human situations. They cherished above all the humorous side of human existence, which when expressed in artistic works always implies a considerable degree of mental development and agility. The whole attitude of the western people gives their works a strong appeal. They speak an eternal language addressed directly to the heart and intellect of everyone who sees them, the intrinsically valuable language of art.

Importance of ceramics

1. CHUPICUARO AND MICHAOCÁN

Olmec influence

It is quite possible that the Olmecs were the earliest forerunners of the artists in the western district, so far as the technical development of ceramics is concerned. These powerful Asiatic people seem to loom in the background everywhere, and one can hardly avoid giving them credit for being the teachers of pottery-making. As a matter of fact, a private collection exists in Mexico City in which

Six Olmec heads. *Above, left and right:* extremely human renderings of the Olmec type. Both actual size. Josué Saenz Collection, Mexico City. *Above, centre:* an interesting head, very early. Feuchtwanger Collection, Mexico City. Height 9 cm. *Below:* pieces from the author's collection. Note the Negroid type on the left. Height: below, left 6.5 cm; centre actual size; right 6 cm. *Cf. p. 124.*

this evolution can be studied step by step, particularly in relation to certain finds in the state of Morelos. A very old tradition may also have seeped through from the culture on the lower reaches of the Balsas River in Guerrero into the region of present-day Michoacán, whence it spread further north. On the other side of this region there must have been contacts between the plateau of Mexico and the westernmost tip of Guanajuato. Proof of this are archaic pieces of Chupicuaro ware which coincide chronologically with the late pre-Classic epoch of the plateau of central Mexico. Great similarities can be found especially with the figurines which were excavated under the lava crust of San Angel near Mexico City.

The lovely 'female' tripod reproduced on page 30 shows the subtle feeling for sculptural forms that these talented ceramists had and their perception for the natural sensuality of the human body. A collection of pretty pieces from Michoacán which are related to those from neighbouring Chupicuaro illustrates this tendency. The three enchanting girls reproduced on page 152 express an essentially coquettish and feminine character with grace, refinement and great naturalness. They also show that the westerners must have been cheerful and affectionate people.

PLATE P. 30

PLATE P. 152

2. NAYARIT AND JALISCO

The most unusual specimens of Mexican clay sculptures are un-doubtedly those found in Nayarit and the adjacent region of Jalisco. The fantasy of the artists seems to have been without bounds. Their continuously developing taste ranged from the most subtle simplifications to the wildest, most 'baroque' creations, even reaching the realm of the bizarre. Some experts are inclined to consider Nayarit almost a madhouse of artistic activity. Yet in spite of all the exaggerations and violent mannerisms (or precisely on account of them), Nayarit forms come very close to certain artistic concepts of

Diversity of Nayarit art

Above: two dancers from Huachin, Veracruz. Height of figure on the left 20 cm; of that on the right 23 cm. *Below:* two fragments which suggest affinities with Maya cultures. Height: of figure on the left 8 cm; of that on the right 9 cm. *Cf. p. 137.*

145

our own age. How distant in time this art is from our own epoch cannot be stated with even approximate assurance. An exception is the case of Chupicuaro, which belongs culturally to the central plateau and must be assigned to the pre-Classic period. One fact admitted by all connoisseurs and archaeologists is that the tenacious continuation of Archaic styles in the western district seems slowly to have become divorced from the general development of neighbouring cultures in the south-east. When we speak of Archaic Nayarit or Archaic Colima ceramics, this must be taken *cum grano salis*, in the sense that we refer more to their general appearance than to any chronological category. E. W. Gifford dates certain specimens from Ixtlan del Rio (Nayarit) to about 1100 AD, thus placing them in the post-Classic era. I believe, however, that the entire western district was host to a series of much earlier artistic activities, probably as far back as pre-Classic times.

PLATE P. 126 The naked old man with a self-contented air reproduced on page 126 can be classified as belonging to the early Nayarit period, whereas the dramatic flautist on his left can be regarded as a late, highly stylized Jalisco figure. A world of evolution lies between them *Semitic type* but the basic idea remains the same: the expression of the Semitic type. Again and again we see the elongated head and the even more elongated nose in Jalisco sculptures. One is forced to admit the intentional emphasis on an ideal of beauty related to a definite racial type.

An intermediate position may be assigned to two other figures: the PLATE P. 158 aristocratic head on page 158 (upper right), as exaggerated vertically as the preceding examples, and the extraordinary clay sculpture shown below. On the latter the application of a light cream-coloured slip served to indicate a fair skin, the tone that many of the inhabitants of the area are reputed to have had before the Spanish conquest. In the handsome head on the left in the top row the refined play of different shades of clay can be seen. The piece is of medium size (18 centimetres) and is curiously reminiscent of the Veracruz school.

PLATE P. 157 Also of outstanding interest are the pieces on page 157. A colourful group of typical Jalisco citizens are shown above, and below are two ingeniously simplified figures from Nayarit. The exquisite colour scheme and the lively aspect of these ceramics display well the subtlety of concept and richness of imagination of which their creators were capable.

A particularly striking figure is the old man with the pointed beard and curved back seated in an Oriental position of meditation (page PLATE P. 171 171). Figures of this type are generally known in Mexico as 'Chinescos'. The specimen shown here seems, however, to represent a rare mixture. The Asiatic and the Semitic types are so convincingly combined and their character so well expressed in this simple clay sculpture that a truly individual personality is the result, even in this western district. Below are two magnificent nudes from Nayarit, unfortunately on a very reduced scale (the one on the left measures 60 centimetres; the one on the right is slightly smaller). Both affirm the extraordinary creative power of the artists, who mastered with playful ease the problems of volume and form. Combined in the same figurine is realistic and abstract detail, producing a charming, original and quite intentional reciprocal effect in the general scheme of composition.

The famous British sculptor, Henry Moore, admits openly to having been attracted and influenced by pre-Columbian art; the same can be said of one of our most distinguished Mexican painters, Rufino Tamayo. It is to be expected that in the future many more artists will join these eminent men in an effort to understand truly the art of ancient America. In my opinion we have only just begun to evaluate and make use of the enormous treasure chest of pre-Columbian art.

Recently another valuable and significant piece from Jalisco has been discovered, now in a private collection in Mexico City. The 'White Lady' on page 127 well illustrates the characteristic style PLATE P. 127 of this western region, which reached such a high level. The distinguished equable features are those of a well-bred, aristocratic woman, and the luxuriantly mature body has been made more interesting by an intentional shortening of the arms. All in all, the work not only suggests the presence of a beautiful white woman in pre-Columbian times, but also demonstrates the astounding ability of ancient Mesoamerican artists to grasp this beauty and to preserve it for posterity in a rich, plastic form.

3. COLIMA

The first thing that comes to our minds when Colima, a relatively small enclave of the western region, is mentioned, are the charming, often-reproduced terracotta dogs. They have caught the fancy of art connoisseurs all over the world because of their great technical and artistic quality. One of the best collections of these lovable animals is that in the newly opened Diego Rivera Museum (Anahuacalli) in Mexico City. The most beautiful example, however, is housed in the Frieda Kahlo Museum in Coyoacán, which is kept open to the public in memory of the wife of the great painter. The Colima people apparently considered their faithful dogs not only indispensable companions during their own lifetime, but also necessary for life after death. Therefore no important Colima burial-place was without an effigy of these charming canines. The predilection and special attention given to dogs underscores the congeniality and delightful character of the people of this region. On the whole it can be said, if such a comparison is permissible, that in their approach to life the western people seem to have come closest to the occidental image of the Homeric epoch. It is no surprise that their representations of human beings in particular should have a lot to tell us.

During the so-called Archaic period (of whose beginning and duration we know so little) interesting and often quite impressive figures

Above: large heads from Veracruz. Classic. Height of both heads 17 cm. That on the left is in the Stiftung Preussischer Kulturbesitz, Staatliche Museen, Berlin-Dahlem; that on the right is in the Kurt Stavenhagen Collection, Mexico City. *Below:* two female dancers. The one on the left shows a Negroid and the one on the right an Asiatic strain. Height: figure on the left 23 cm; that on the right 22 cm. The former is in the Kurt Stavenhagen Collection, Mexico City; the latter is in the collection of the author. There is a striking resemblance between the figure *below, left* and the well-known ebony head of the Egyptian queen Tiy, the Negroid mother of Tutenkhamen. See I. Woldering, *Egypt*, ART OF THE WORLD series, p. 162. *Cf. p. 139.*

Four more portrait heads from Veracruz. Those on top are smaller, those below of medium size. Height of heads above, left and right: 9 cm, 10.5 cm; of those below 12.5 cm, 14 cm. From various private collections in Mexico. *Cf. p. 141.*

Superb Classic head from Veracruz. Kurt Stavenhagen Collection, Mexico City. Height 23 cm.
Cf. p. 141.

were produced. With their simple and direct language they convey precisely the same kind of universal meaning and validity that we are accustomed to attach to the poetic works of Homer.

A few intriguing faces can be seen on page 172, reproduced in PLATE P. 172 colour. The close-up view on the left (upper row) shows the head of a sturdy warrior wearing a horn-studded helmet. He reminds us in a strange but not implausible way of a Viking, who might have strolled from Virginia to Colima! As far as the charming girl on the right is concerned, the similarity between her face and that of the typical North American girl of today is startling. The impertinent, uncomplicated handling of the eye form, which well suits this energetic but prim American maiden, is another demonstration of the outstanding natural talent of pre-Columbian artists. The double figure at the bottom of the photograph is a real Colima masterpiece. Its simple design is in complete harmony with the intense, powerful and somewhat mysterious sentiment evident between the two figures. This is a quality achieved only with difficulty in the realm of sculpture: that almost indefinable fluidum that exists in the inner relationship of two human beings.

The representations of the human body modelled by the Colima artists exist in innumerable varieties of position, mood and gesture. A small selection is shown on page 128. On the left side (upper row) an 'Archaic' figure radiates a natural humaneness that is not easily explained verbally. Next to it is a 'situation' picture of convincing excellence. The artist has not attempted to show any tragic problems of over-population, child welfare or food shortage, but simply a good-natured, naturally prolific mother, depicted in a humorous, cheerful way. I propose that this completely natural human being be elevated to the rank of a 'goddess' of fertility, for the benefit of those who are bent on finding deities! Another 'divine' occupation could be given to the figure on the lower right-hand side. It is impossible to imagine a more strictly human situation; this little man

Above: 'Three Graces' from Michoacán. *Below:* 'Witch' from Nayarit. Pre-Classic period. Private collection, Barcelona. Height: figure above 11 cm; figure below 15 cm. *Cf. p. 145.*

153

is so pensive, so peaceful and satisfied, a veritable artistic egg of Columbus! The figure on the lower left is completely of another sort, and its dramatic element immediately stirs the emotions of the viewer. The mother bewailing her dead or sick child is a touching, tragic figure. The full impact cannot be realized from a photograph but is very powerful when one sees the actual sculpture. The expressive entanglement of the limbs gives a better idea of the sad event than might have been achieved simply by means of a distorted facial expression.

PLATE P. 173 Another whole figure, shown in colour on page 173, captures yet another situation in clay. The subject, a little boy with a jar that is too heavy for him, has been given a masterful interpretation. The splendid ceramic technique employed and the form and expression embodied in the piece could almost symbolize the usually friendly and happy mood of the artists of Colima. Far away is any modern thought of an overburdened, misused child or any fanatic, tragic complex of the last post-Classic Aztecs... oh happy world of the West!

VI. THE MAYA REGION

The artistic greatness of the Mayas was acknowledged by the cultivated world much earlier than was that of other pre-Columbian cultures. The imposing architecture of the sacred Maya temple cities is famous, both those from the first Classic era (found in the regions between Chiapas, Mexico and Honduras, including Guatemala) and those from the second post-Classic era (found on the Yucatán Peninsula). Also renowned are the marvellous reliefs and sculptures in stone and stucco which abound in all the Maya regions and which practically always represent human beings. They range from huge solitary stelae, covered with glyptic inscriptions and decorations as framework for one big expressive head in the central part, to finely chiselled low reliefs of priests in ceremonial poses, such as the splendid Jonuta stone in the National Museum of Mexico. In this context of human portraiture I should like to mention particularly the magnificent stucco mask of a most spiritual elderly personage, at present also in the National Museum of Anthropology in Mexico City (reproduced in colour in *Vergleichende Weltgeschichte* by Hans Hofstätter and Hannes Pixa, Baden-Baden, 1964, vol. 8, page 79) and last but not least the two famous stucco heads in the tomb of Palenque—prototypes of the utter refinement of highly bred young men, both in physical looks and extremely elegant attire. All these pieces represent the world of the aristocracy, the system of careful selection and the oligarchic government of priestly rulers. Some express the remarkable inner concentration of a sage, as precisely the above-mentioned mask; others are less introverted but intellectually alive and often of haughtily superior appearance. All of them are very human and must have been, each in his own way, great personalities of ancient America known to the artists who immortalized them. For this reason they fit nicely into the general framework of our investigations.

Since the Maya were highly accomplished in fresco-painting as well as architecture and sculpture, it does not seem surprising that they should also have produced extraordinary works in the field of ceramics. Less familiar are their older and more primitive ceramics, of which greater quantities will probably be found in the future. Perhaps they have been overlooked or else have been regarded as uninteresting by excavators and collectors because they were not considered 'pretty' enough.

Earliest ceramics

PLATE P. 163 Illustrated here are two pieces of primitive ceramic from the Maya region. Above, on the right, is an incense-burner of unusual interest. Its two ears, including the ear-plugs, form a double profile of the face, which covers the whole urn, so that the vessel has not one but three distinct noses. The piece is of great strength and beauty, and exudes the atmosphere of an ancient sacred ceremony. A piece similar to this from Monte Albán III is now in the collection of the National Museum of Anthropology in Mexico City. On the extreme left is another ceramic, thematically related to the first piece. It looks as if it might be the priest who performed ceremonies with the incense-burner!

In contrast to these two pieces is the figure between them, a distinguished lady of the late Classic epoch with an oddly fashioned but extremely elegant hat. Below is a close-up of a famous Maya figure from Jaina Island near Campeche, from the Robert Woods Bliss Collection in Washington, D. C. This is one of the finest and most refined human representations in clay sculpture from the pre-Columbian world. We have already come across a double-figure ceramic from Colima which exhibits a sensitive relationship between the figures, and the Jaina piece displays this same maturity of concept and execution.

Late Classic figures

At the beginning of this chapter I mentioned the ability of the Maya in a variety of artistic disciplines, including fresco-painting. It would be a grave omission if a sample of Maya ceramic-painting

Superb ensemble from Jalisco *(above)* and Nayarit *(below)*. Typical style of the western region, which shows that the pre-Classic (Archaic) concept probably survived to the post-Classic period. Group above slightly reduced; group below actual size. *Cf. p. 146.*

were not included in this publication, and on page 174 is a very PLATE P. 174 representative and interesting example. Dating from the late Classic period, it was found in Campeche and represents a lady with a flower. The fascinating coiffure, the spirited agile limbs and the whole stylish deportment of this elegant woman are not only amazing, but also significant in that they indicate the high level of Maya culture. The figure has an undeniable Negroid character and also a certain affinity with Egyptian painting. On viewing this picture for the first time the well-known Mexican poet Carlos Pellicer remarked: 'Even the lotus flower reminds us of the Nile!'

In this chapter on Maya ceramics I must also include a showpiece PLATES PP. 164, 165 of the Musée de l'Homme in Paris, an incense-burner discovered in Guatemala, probably from the Classic period. It is adorned with a magnificent head and on account of its size and excellent condition is one of the most noble pieces of ancient American clay sculpture. I doubt whether any art historian in the world, if he viewed its almost biblical features without knowing its origin, would assign this piece to pre-Columbian America. Yet it is one of the 'silent' but extremely audible voices of the New World.

These heads from Nayarit *(above, left)* and Jalisco *(above, right and below)* are full of character and convey magnificently a noble human type. Height: above, left 18 cm; above, right 24 cm; below 30 cm. *Cf. p. 146.*

VII. CONNECTIONS WITH EL SALVADOR, COLOMBIA AND ECUADOR; AND A BRIEF GLIMPSE AT THE REST OF THE WORLD

Contacts along Pacific coast

The relationships between Mesoamerica and South America in pre-Columbian times have not been very thoroughly explored. It is certain, however, that there were contacts between these areas and that the route of connection ran along the Pacific coast.*

These connections are confirmed by Spanish historical sources from the sixteenth century. Contact certainly existed during the pre-Classic period between Guerrero and El Salvador: witness the two

PLATE P. 166   Salvadorian heads on page 166 (*b* and *d*). The Negroid one is from a private collection in Paris and the one above is from the Museum für Völkerkunde in Berlin-Dahlem. Both are in exactly the same style as many of the pieces from Guerrero reproduced in this book and exhibit peculiarly elongated hats and the exaggerated vertical form. But even more surprising, on account of the enormous distances involved, are the pieces from the Tumaco culture, located on a promontory of the Pacific coast in northern Ecuador and southern Colombia.

PLATE P. 166   The piece shown on page 166 in the left centre (*c*) is reproduced with the gracious permission of the National Museum in Bogotá. It represents a man with a noble profile and a lofty bearing, wearing the same type of head-dress as the woman directly above, a figure found in Guerrero. In the bottom row of the same photograph appear four fine pieces from Esmeraldas and Manabí, both on the

Ecuadorian works   coast of Ecuador. The dignified man on the right, with the pointed beard, belongs to the Museum für Völkerkunde in Vienna, as does the incredible and unique double-bearded man (*f*). The other two pieces, attractive girls with a typical kind of hood, are from the Museum für Völkerkunde in Hamburg. My sincere thanks are due to the amiable Director of the Vienna museum, Frau Dr. Becker-

---

* Alfred Kidder II, 'Rediscovering America', *Horizon*, 1964; an interesting article which deals with the latest research work by Estrada, Evans and Meggers.

FIG. 15 – *Small clay sculpture, modelled with the utmost care, in which certain affinities with Meso-america cannot be overlooked. From Ecuador. Actual size. Private collection of S. Hirtz, Quito.*

Donner, and to my admired friend and meritorious professor, Franz Termer of Hamburg, for their help in securing photographs of these Ecuadorian pieces. The remarkable thing about the connections between Ecuador and Mexico is not that the Esmeraldas and Manabí heads bear great similarity to Maya pieces, with which they are frequently compared, but that (enigma of enigmas!) they are so much like the terracottas of the Huasteca!

The next two pages of black-and-white illustrations demonstrate clearly the early Ecuadorian artist's urge to portray his contemporaries in a realistic manner. This interest may have led to the development of the famous Mochica portrait vessels, or at least may have been an influence on the Peruvian ceramics which have been so widely published in every book on American art history and were also dealt with by H.-D. Disselhoff in the first volume on ancient America of the ART OF THE WORLD series. For this reason I have not included illustrations of Mochica ware in this book, although they were decidedly important elements in the 'human image of the New World' in pre-hispanic days.*

PLATES PP. 179, 180

Mochica portrait vessels

Far less well known are the clay sculptures of the Esmeraldas and Manabí region on the Pacific coast of Ecuador. The bust of an

PLATE P. 180

Esmeraldas and Manabí

* The best examples of these unusually beautiful heads were published by Ubbelohde-Doering in his book *The Art of Ancient Peru*, New York, 1954.

161

PLATE P. 180 enchanting girl, reproduced here in its actual size, invites us to imagine the presentation of a bride. The head-dress and the triangular mark are remarkable for their 'Phoenician' affinities. This very valuable piece belongs to the archaeological collection of the Central Bank of Quito, whose director, Sr. Hernán Crespo, kindly allowed me to photograph it. The other Ecuadorian heads (mainly from Manabí) are from private collections in Quito and Mexico. Many of them show definite Semitic features, particularly the mask PLATE P. 179 shown on page 179, which has been included here on account of its lively and human expression. Below this mask is a very rare, powerfully modelled Negroid head, another indication of early mixtures in South America.

Colombia: gold pieces The most beautiful and literally the most valuable Negroid representation from pre-hispanic America belongs to Colombia and can be found in the second showcase of the famous Gold Museum (Museo de Oro) of the National Bank in Bogotá. The piece measures 17 centimetres in height and is of gold with a light copper alloy. It FIG. 16 was reproduced in colour in 1948 in the bank's catalogue of the museum. Our drawing gives an idea of the appearance of the face and form of this unusual figure. Extremely interesting—apart from the Negro physiognomy of the face— are the neck-rings in African style. The strange box-like set of teeth has a surprising parallel in

Page 163: Maya terracottas. *(a)*: early figure of a bearded man. Private collection, Zurich. Height about 15 cm. *(b)*: later mould-cast figure. National Museum, Mexico City. An outstanding feature is the natural elegance and simplicity of the modelling. Note also the peculiarly 'Etruscan', even 'proto-Etruscan' headgear. *(c)*: pre-Classic incense-burner. *(d)*: outstanding human rendering of a well-known Jaina figure. From the Bliss Collection, Washington, D. C. Slightly enlarged. *Cf. p. 156.*

Page 164: Magnificent incense-burner from the Maya zone at Iximche near Chimaltenango, Guatemala. Probably early Classic and related to similar incense-burners from Veracruz. Height 33.5 cm. Musée de l'Homme, Paris. *Cf. p. 159.*

Page 165: Bold profile of a man, almost Biblical in character, which takes up the front of the incense-burner. The kinship with Mediterranean cultures is undeniable. Actual size. *Cf. p. 159.*

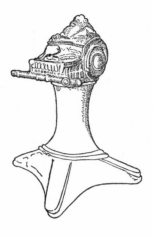

two small terracotta heads on exhibit in the main Teotihuacán showcase of the Diego Rivera Museum in Mexico City. In regard to the early appearance of Negroid elements in the pre-Columbian art of South America, the comments of the Spanish Dominican monk, Fray Gregorio García, acquire renewed interest. According to Fray García, who spent nine years in Peru in the sixteenth century, the Spaniards saw Negroes for the first time in the New World on an island off the shore of Cartagena, Colombia. He wrote as follows: 'Aqui se hallaron Esclavos del Señor, Negros, que fueron los primeros, que los nuestros vieron en las Indias'.*

Another piece which depicts a Negroid personality, equal in value to the example in the gold collection of the National Bank in Bogotá, is the well-known gold pectoral of the National Museum of Anthropology in Mexico City, commonly considered Mixtec although it was discovered at Papantla, Veracruz. Erroneously this piece has been considered a representation of Huehuetéotl, the 'old' or 'fire' god, probably because a few filigree gold threads form a skimpy beard on his face! This opinion was recently voiced by

FIG. 17

---

* Fray Gregorio García, *Orígen de los Indios del Nuevo Mundo*, libr. 3, cap. I., fol. 238.

(a): very rare figure with South American affinities, found in the coastal area of Guerrero. Height about 9 cm. I. Peters Collection. *(c):* a fine example in the Museum at Bogotá. From Tumaco, southern Colombia (bordering on the province of Esmeraldas in Ecuador). Height about 16 cm. *(b), (d):* pre-Classic heads from the Pacific coast of El Salvador. *(b)* is a white type, *(d)* a Negroid one. Height: *(c)* 10 cm; *(d)* 11 cm. Staatliche Museen, Berlin-Dahlem and private collection, Paris. *(e), (f), (g), (h):* pre-Classic figurines of European character from Esmeraldas and Manabí (Ecuador). *(e):* woman wearing a head-cloth. Height about 7 cm. Völkerkundemuseum, Hamburg. *(f):* man with (very rare!) double beard. Height about 6 cm. Völkerkundemuseum, Vienna. *(g):* girl with head-cloth projecting to the rear (or possibly with a deformation of the head). Height about 7 cm. Völkerkundemuseum, Hamburg. *(h):* man with pointed beard. Völkerkundemuseum, Vienna. *Cf. p. 160.*

FIGS. 17, 18 – *Above: gold pectoral. Height 15 cm. National Museum, Mexico City. Below: gold pendant. Height 15 cm. Mixteca Alta, Coixtlahuaca, Oaxaca.*

Raul Flores Guerrero in his *Historia General del Arte Mexicano*.* If one wants to give a 'divine' Nahuatl name to this pectoral, one should at least use the more correct designation of Naualpilli, in later epochs the deity of goldsmiths and jewellers, who in other representations also exhibits Negroid characteristics (see footnote on page 96 and caption to Plate on page 149). An entirely different meaning can be attached to the gold pendant found in the Mixteca Alta (Coixtlahuaca, Oaxaca), which probably does represent the fire god. Actually in this piece we are again confronted with our old friend, the early Semitic immigrant, who is probably at the source of all the 'fire gods', 'old gods' and ancient incense-burners of pre-Columbian America. In the case of the Coixtlahuaca find, a connection with the earlier Colombian gold pectorals has undoubtedly to be accepted. The two Mexican pieces are shown in

FIGS. 17, 18 — adjoining drawings to illustrate vividly once again the two racial types which, as has often been mentioned, were probably representations of the most important ancient American personalities.

The interesting Negro described above is not, however, the only figure of value for our study from the glittering treasure-house of

Quimbaya portraits in gold — Colombia, for we also find here an impressive supply of Semitic types, likewise in pure gold. Their presence was made known (and indeed famous) by the bank's publication previously mentioned,

* Mexico City, 1962, plate 91, page 138.

168

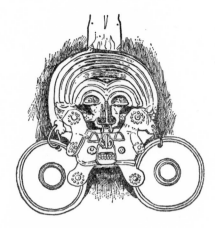

and by the de luxe edition on the gold treasure of Bogotá by José
Pérez de Barradas (Madrid, 1954). When I visited the Gold Museum
in 1964 I confirmed my impression of these pieces, and the adjoining
drawings will convey them to the reader. They also show that many   FIGS. 19–24
significant 'human images of the New World' appeared on the South
American continent.

Figures 19, 20 and 21 evoke the primeval or ancestral dignity of the   FIGS. 19–21
Old Testament. The more physical, human aspect of these ancient
personalities who must have had so much influence in America is
emphasized in Figures 22 and 23. In the 'needle head' of Figure 24   FIGS. 22–23
even an exaggeratedly grotesque line comes to the fore.

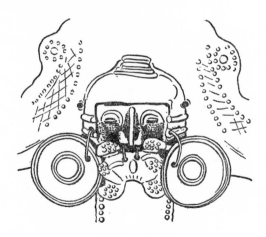

FIGS. 19–21: *Above, left: pectoral. Colima.*
Above, right and below: ornaments. All of
these are renderings of objects in the Museo
del Oro, Bogotá.

169

PLATES PP. 164,
165

PLATE P. 180

All the examples shown here, including the Negro, are products of the Quimbaya culture in the Cauca valley of Colombia, which apparently flourished between 400 and 600 AD, and thus belongs to the Classic epoch. There might even be a relationship between these pieces and the magnificent Guatemalan incense-burner reproduced on pages 164 and 165. Earlier forerunners of the Columbian gold figures can be sought in remains from the Tumaco and Esmeraldas cultures. A plausible example is the hypothetically arranged family tree of the pretty girl from Quito. Again and again we see not only the duality of the leading personalities of America, but in the latter items the physically effective leaven of a powerful race, which evidently penetrated – if only in small quantities – a large part of the American continent in early times.

Terracottas in Old World: Phoenician

For the sake of comparison it is interesting for the art historian to examine the terracotta production of various other cultures of the world and note similarities between their technique, style and content and those of the clay figures of the Americas. First we might

Three figures from Nayarit. *Above:* fine example of the so-called 'Chinesco' type with beard and a Semitic strain. Height 17 cm. *Below:* these two figures are indicative of the superb skill with which artists of the western region conceived the human body. Height: figure on the left 60 cm; that on the right 57 cm. *Cf. p. 147.*

Figures from Colima executed in the ancient style. Note the horned helmet of the man *(above, left)* and the European style of the woman *(above, right)*. Height: figure above, left 18 cm; that above, right 12 cm; that below 21 cm. *Cf. p. 153.*

Boy carrying a jar. Figurine from Colima. About actual size. Private collection, Barcelona. *Cf. p. 154.* →

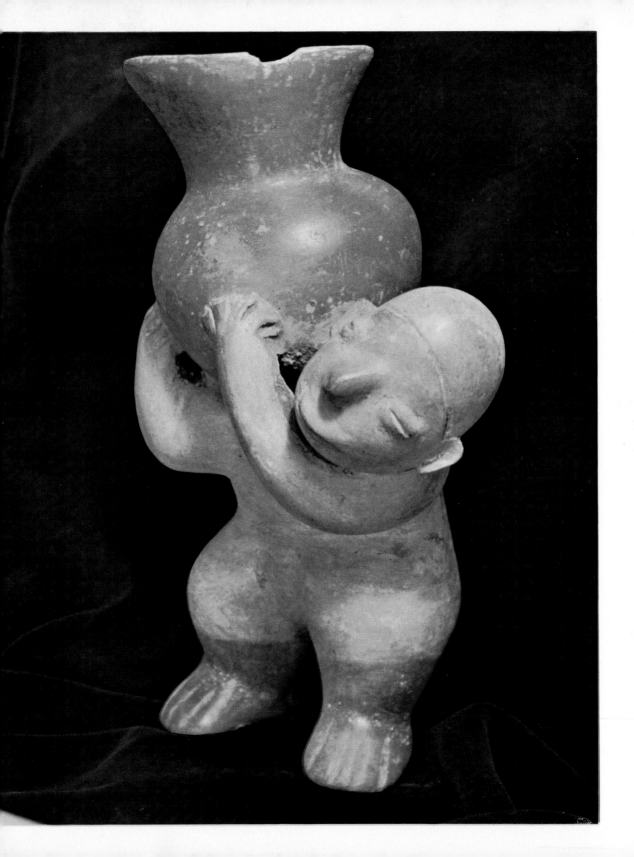

Maya plate. Late Classic. Actual size. Private collection of Manuel Barbachano, Mexico City. *Cf. p. 159.*

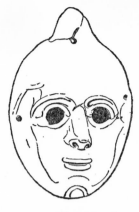 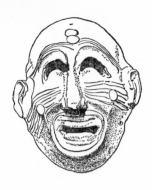

FIG. 25 – *Phoenician clay mask from the necropolis at Cadiz, Spain. Height about 13 cm. After a photograph by the author.*
FIG. 26 – *Phoenician clay mask from Carthage. Approx. 7th century BC. Height about 15 cm. Louvre, Paris.*

examine the Mediterranean area, where so many beautiful terra-cotta pieces were produced. Wherever the Phoenicians went – and they went almost everywhere – human beings modelled in clay can be found. They have been discovered from Cadiz and Ibiza to Tyre and from Cyprus to Carthage. In Cadiz I found some very inter-esting clay masks in the storeroom of the local museum, including one with Negroid features. The best Punic mask, however, is proba-bly the one in the Louvre in Paris. This piece was excavated in FIG. 26 Carthage, but if it had been found or were even merely exhibited in Mexico would immediately be classified as a kind of Huehuetéotl (fire god)! In reality this mask is connected with the cult of Hum-baba, a Phoenician deity, guardian of the forest of Lebanon, the most ancient prototype of which originated in Ur (and is now in the British Museum).*

On my latest research trip to the Mediterranean (1966) I was able to confirm the fact that no Phoenician excavation site (Ibiza, Cag-

* See Sidney Smith, 'The Face of Humbaba', *Annals of Prehistoric Archaeology and Anthropology*, Liverpool, vol. XI, 1900, and Joan Boardmann, *The Greeks Overseas*, 1964. The opinion of T. A. Joyce of the British Museum quoted by Smith does not seem quite correct to me, since the representation of Humbaba was certainly transported around, not only to Samos and Sparta (I saw specimens of Humbaba from Sparta myself in the Ashmolean Museum in Oxford), but apparently also all over the Mediterranean and even to America!

liari, Tunis, Motya in Sicily etc.) is without a representation of this type of figure. A specimen from Cagliari is especially interesting, as a simile of it appeared as far away as Nigeria in Africa, where it was discovered by the famous German explorer, Leo Frobenius. The French investigators Gilbert and Colette Charles-Picard, known for their book on life in Carthage (*La Vie quotidienne à Carthage*), are preparing a publication on Phoenician masks which will certainly give us a new insight into this important aspect of art history.

The complexes of Mycenae and Cyprus are likely to show many parallels, particularly Cyprus with its entangled mixture of Greek and Oriental (chiefly Phoenician) influences. Anyone who studies the important standard treatise of Franz Winter on ancient terracottas can distinguish very quickly, without looking at the captions, which pieces come from the mainland of Europe and which come from Asia Minor. The Antikensammlung in Berlin includes a large number of very fine clay sculptures, some of which were described in a small book by Gerda Bruns (1946). As well as reproducing some elegant Tanagra figures of the Greek Coroplastes, she also shows a few excellent facial studies. One of these is a female head from Crete; another is one of the best frontal clay bricks of Etruria, a region where a great number of parallels are found with Mesoamerican items.

Etruscan The study of Etruscan art is also extremely instructive, as it illustrates the continuous interaction between Greek and Italian cultural developments and also shows the connections with the territories within the Phoenician orbit. In the Antikensammlung in Munich FIG. 27 there is a wonderful wine jar of purely Greek ceramic technique. In the artistic execution, however, the Greek element was reduced to a wreath of leaves on the top and a little Silenus mask on the back, whereas the entire vessel is taken up by a Phoenician head. I do not know if the red glass pearl, now fastened by a golden wire to the hooked nose, is original or not. In any case, it would be an interesting addition since the vessel undoubtedly had to do with the importation of red wine, which was shipped in great quantities from Carthage in exchange for Etrurian metals. The nose pearl is also a very noticeable feature of a number of early terracotta

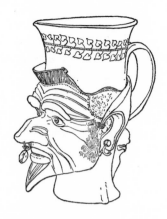

faces from Mesoamerica. Another wine jar, equally interesting, can be found in the Etruscan collection of the Vatican Museum. It has been formed from not one but two heads and obviously pokes fun at both the Semitic and the stubby Greek nose (style of Socrates). The Etruscans were certainly not lacking a sense of humour...

Another significant late Mediterranean terracotta in the Berlin collection is the magnificent head of a girl from Tarentum. Gerda Bruns, the author of the book mentioned above, correctly declares that this terracotta of the early part of the first century AD represents a Greek girl, which is interesting since it belongs in every respect to the Roman portrait school and can even be classified as one of its masterpieces. This shows clearly how a talented artist can produce —by concentrated effort—the image of a real person, presenting in essence subtly indicated racial characteristics.

The well-known Egyptian terracottas of Africa are of great impor- *Egyptian* tance. They depict a wealth of human traits which must have pertained to the inhabitants of the banks of the Nile during the long history of this ancient nation. In other widely separated regions of the African continent many points of comparison can be found which are also worth mentioning: for instance, the ancient dramatic ceramics of the Chad area and the very early, boldly modelled Nok figurines which, in all probability, were the embryo from which the brilliant works of Ife and Benin later developed. It is curious that certain Veracruz clay sculptures in the museum at Jalapa which exhibit strong Negroid traits show the use of a similar eye technique: a straight upper line and a decidedly curved lower line. Exactly the contrary is the case in Manabí, Ecuador, and in very early Greek figures. Recently in the western part of Africa there have *West African* appeared clay sculptures of great interest, such as the splendid head lately acquired by the Italian Government from the Rovayroux collection in Dakar. During the time of my exhibition of photographs and terracottas of pre-Columbian Negroid representations in Dakar in April 1966 (at the First World Festival of Negro Art), I was able to admire and to photograph some exceptional Ashanti terracottas which have a striking similarity to certain works from Veracruz, both in technique and in artistic content.

Near Eastern The third region of importance for comparative studies of terracottas is that comprising the countries which became famous in antiquity because of the campaigns of Alexander the Great. As a point of departure we might mention the pioneering work of Theodor Bossert, whose excellent book on ancient Syria includes many intriguing illustrations of clay sculptures. Farther east is Baluchistan

Page 179: Various South American specimens from the Manabí and Esmeraldas cultures of Ecuador, all of which may be ascribed to the pre-Classic period. The clay mask is reminiscent of a fine stylized head in the National Museum at Bogotá and generally speaking of many similar Mesoamerican ones. *(d)* represents the Negroid element in Ecuador. Height: *(a)* 9.5 cm; *(b)*, *(c)* 6 cm; *(d)*, *(e)* 8 cm. *Cf. p. 161.*

Page 180: *Left (a)*: one of the finest clay sculptures of the pre-Classic Esmeraldas culture in Ecuador, possibly representing a (Phoenician?) bride. *Right:* of these four heads the three upper ones are likewise from the Esmeraldas peninsula and the bottom one is executed in the style of nearby Manabí; they give the impression of being a 'row of ancestors', the four grandparents of the bride! Height: about actual size; *(b)* 7 cm; *(c)* 7 cm; *(d)* 6.5 cm; *(e)* 7 cm. *Cf. pp. 161, 170.*

Page 181: Interesting juxtaposition of objects illustrating the inexhaustible wealth of Mexico. *(a)*: fragment of a Huasteca clay sculpture with Etruscan decoration of the helmet, obviously representing a white man. Late Classic. Height 8.5 cm. *(b)*: monumental head of a clay vessel measuring one metre in height. State Museum, Jalapa, Veracruz. A. Medellin regards this as an Olmec find. We are thus once again confronted with the great Semitic counterpart of the Asiatic-African master race. Height about 18 cm. *(c)*: a Mixtec Negro head, post-Classic, which I have only recently 'discovered' in one of the storage-rooms of the new National Museum in Mexico City, following up a clue given by C. Nuñez, the Mexican codex scholar. This interesting figure, 14 cm high, is stored among hundreds of *mexica* (Aztec objects), since it was found on the plateau of Mexico during excavations of Aztec strata. According to C. Nuñez this figure was probably venerated by the Aztecs as Tezcatlipoca for the simple reason that it was black, and thus had the 'correct' colour for this deity. *(d)*: Negroid 'Silenus mask', by the hand of an Olmec master. From Tlatilco. Pre-Classic. Height 16 cm. *(Cf. footnote on p. 49).*

b

c

e

a

b

c

d

e

b

d

1550 1564

(studied by Heinz Mode, of Halle-on-Saale) and north of Kashmir lies Khotan, another site where some interesting clay figures have been discovered, a small collection of which is now in the Berlin-Dahlem Museum. These pieces were transferred to Berlin after the return of the Prussian expedition to Turfan before the First World War. The noble Semitic faces of these small terracottas* remind one of the historical fact that Phoenician merchants participated in the expedition of the great Macedonian. Alexander's enterprise pushed a variety of ethnic groups into the remote eastern areas of his expeditions. It is still a mystery what became of his admiral, Nearchus (who furnished us with a wonderfully correct 'log book' of the coastline of the Arabian Sea), and to the crew of his ship, which consisted in all probability of a very motley crowd of human elements.

The ancient ceramics of India are full of interesting parallels with the ones produced in Mesoamerica, and anyone acquainted with

Indian and Far Eastern

* I do not know if these Semitic types could be related to the 'white' and 'black' Jews who settled in India (Kachin) in ancient times, according to Emil Schmidt ('Beiträge zur Antropologie Südindiens', *Archiv für Anthropologie*, Brunswick, 1910).

Explanation of the 14 illustrations in the *Códice Sierra*, which comes from Santiago Tejupa near Teposcolula (Oaxaca) and was compiled between the years 1550 and 1564. *Left-hand column*, reading from top to bottom: *(i)*: clerical banner with tithe. The coin with a cross *(above, right and below, left)* denotes 20 gold pesos of the day; the coin *below, right* with an '8' denotes 1 peso (= 8 reales). *(ii)* expenditure of the community for the church bell. The spiral with the feather denotes 400 gold pesos of the day. *(iii)* 60 pesos and 4 reales were spent on the banquet for the priest (Señor Vicario). *Middle column*, reading from top to bottom: *(i)* Nahuatl glyph for the year 1561. *(ii)* burgomaster, clerk and translator *(nahuatlista)*. *(iii)* three Spaniards, on the left the interpreter with the symbol for language, in the centre the governor, Enriquez, and on the right the clerk. *(iv)* 44 pesos were paid to four shepherds for looking after the sheep of the parish. *(v)* 15 pesos was the price of the meal consumed by the burgomaster, clerk and interpreter (note the 16th-century egg-cup!). *Right-hand column*, reading from top to bottom: *(i)* Spaniard counting out money. *(ii)* Marcos Franco, the clerk. *(iii)* in 1564 building work on the church ceased because the parish had to hand over 870 pesos to the central government in Mexico City. The index finger indicating the power of the state and the little head of the Indian taxpayer are superb. *(iv)* once again a lavish meal for a Spaniard, which cost 42 pesos. *(v)* in 1558 440 pesos were taken from the treasure-chest to pay for building work. *Cf. p. 185.*

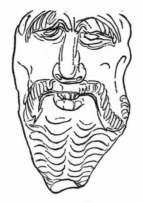

FIGS. 28, 29 – *Above: terracotta head. Nok culture, Nigeria. Before the beginning of the Christian era. From the book by William Fagg. Below: terracotta Semitic head from Khotan. (Turfan Expedition.) Berlin-Dahlem Museum.*

Mexican pieces also feels 'at home' with pieces from Siam. The surprising affinities with early Japanese ceramics have already been mentioned in detail; it remains only to point out the charming clay figurines from Java, which are not easily found in Europe. I succeeded in seeing some of these small terracottas in the University Museums in Zurich and in Amsterdam. Several pieces from the latter collection are strongly reminiscent of Mesoamerican work.

FINAL NOTE: THE CÓDICE SIERRA

INDIAN PORTRAITURE OF THE EARLY POST-COLUMBIAN PERIOD

After the Spanish conquest of Mexico the artistic activities of the Indians were not immediately wiped out. In many instances the inherent creative force of the American natives was expressed in early colonial architecture, sculpture and painting. However, the clearest manifestation of the continuation of pre-hispanic art can be followed in the so-called post-Columbian codices. In these picture books the Indians continued to note down customs and events and frequently wrote passages in their native language with European letters. One of the most interesting and curiously unknown specimens is the Códice Sierra, which was compiled between 1550 and 1564 in Santiago Tejupa near Teposcolula (Oaxaca) and has been thoroughly studied by the distinguished Mexican scholar, Nicolás León. The manuscript, now in Puebla, can be assigned to the Nahuatl group of Popolacas, who settled in a region otherwise occupied by Zapotecs and Mixtecs. That is the reason why the style and in fact the entire concept of the document is preponderantly Aztec. It will be very difficult to find another list of treasurer's expenditures which would, in such an artistic manner, hand down to posterity the why and wherefore of the expenditure of community money. It makes no difference whether objects, animals, people or general situations are treated; everything is shown in a clear and precise manner. With just a few lines the artist conveyed a vivid and convincing image of real European people (in this case with distinctly Spanish characteristics), as he saw them and as we are able to imagine them. His crisp clever drawing seems to jump ahead several centuries and anticipate our modern views and feelings, much more than does anything else produced during the same epoch in the Old World. The will to portray the images of the new human types who suddenly made their appearance in America had not been extinguished!

185

CONCLUSION

Role of religious
element A few years ago William Spratling published a little book about Totonac clay sculpture, with an introduction by Gordon Eckholm, entitled *More Human than Divine*. It is a good title and a good beginning, but that is not enough. To the 'human' we have here added 'man'. The tendency of deify all the artistic endeavours of ancient America, apparent in almost all present-day literature, has in my opinion gone too far. It may be a 'cover-up solution' in the case of material that is insufficiently familiar. There is no doubt that religious attitudes and a well-stocked pantheon of deities played a very important role, especially in the later theocratically organized communities of Mesoamerica. However, in the artistic production of the whole pre-Columbian period these strictly religious representations were not everything. Of course it is fairly simple to register any figure with a beard under the heading Xiuhtecutli or Huehuetéotl, the Nahuatl name for the 'fire' or 'old' god. Utilizing this tempting device further, one can forget that the real question is not so much whether a figure does or does not represent a 'fire god', but to explain the presence of a beard (which real Indians do not have) as a symbol of this deity and why most representations of this kind show decidedly Semitic characteristics.

I am fully aware that by attempting here to employ the artistic instincts and keen observations of pre-Columbian terracotta artists to bring a little more light into the unknown human side of ancient American history, only a first and possibly small step has been made. Yet I believe that this step is a very necessary one in the right direction, particularly when we take into consideration that due to the lack of written records no other alternative is open to us. I am convinced that the many millions of representations of human faces will be able to tell us a great deal, once they have been thoroughly studied.

'Voices of silence' Sometimes these 'voices of silence' are slightly confusing, but some-

times they are clear and distinctly recognizable. To be sure, not every pre-Columbian terracotta is a significant work of art. The vast majority of them were mass-produced works. Of the hundreds of thousands of clay heads which I have held in my hands, only a small percentage had sufficient quality to be illuminating. In those pieces where there is evidence of a strong creative will, a bright ray of cognition comes forth to the viewer, its strength increasing in perspective depth according to the artistic quality and human value of the piece.

I believe that a real artist is capable of producing a truthful image in accordance with the essential facts of life. Some might take offence that this artistic power has been extended to the recognition of racial differentiations, but this point of view is justified, I believe, by the material presented in this book. The representation of white types is so frequent that no one can remain unaware of them. The Negroid element is the exception, but is well proven by the large Olmec stone monuments as well as the terracotta items and therefore cannot be excluded from the pre-Columbian history of the Americas. Furthermore, it is precisely the Negroid representations which often indicate personalities of high position, who can unhesitatingly be compared to the outstanding Negroes who served as models for great works of art in Egypt and in Nigeria. *Representation of racial types*

After having read my two papers on this subject at the International Congress of Americanists in Barcelona on August 31, 1964, I was opposed by an American anthropologist, who declared that all the photographic slides shown in my lecture were the result of 'stylizations' made by Indians. *Art history and anthropology*

I have great respect for the work of anthropologists and may even claim to understand their activities. Yet it might be desirable if some anthropologists occasionally would make an effort to understand that an art historian may be just as intent on searching for the truth as his colleagues who take an anthropological point of view.

The ageing Rembrandt was able to paint his famous picture of two Negroes (1661), now in the Mauritshuis in The Hague, because he was familiar with those two members of the Negro race. If instead of painting them he had measured their skulls and bones, he might

187

have succeeded in becoming an anthropologist but would probably have ceased to be an artist. He managed to give us, by virtue of his marvellous artistic insight, one of the most splendid and true-to-life representations in existence of the Negro race – expressing both its physical and its psychic aspects. As this great artist depicted real people in his paintings, so did Cranach and Dürer show us the essence of German types and so did El Greco manage to transmit to posterity—in spite of vertical stylizations—the most Spanish Spaniards imaginable. In the same way the early American terracotta artists were able to create—and have thus handed down—images of real Mesoamericans. In accordance with this method of reasoning I propose that we put aside the doubts and worries of anthropologists and ethnologists and allow the terracotta works themselves to tell us their story. The creative hands of artists from those ancient days have stretched out to guide us to a new and clearer understanding of the history of the Americas, where apparently not only East and West but in fact the whole world met, a long, long time ago.*

The meaning of all this can be demonstrated by just two illustrations in this book: colour plate 36 and the black-and-white plate on page 181. A close examination and thorough contemplation of these newly discovered witnesses of hitherto unknown human images of ancient America is strongly recommended to the attentive and sensitive reader.**

* The best modern philosophical exposition of the problems of human events as they actually took place on the American continent has in my opinion been sketched by F. S. C. Northrop of Yale University in his book *The Meeting of East and West: an Inquiry Concerning World Understanding*, 1947 (see p.459).

** The racial problem of the early inhabitants of America did not escape the keen intuition and strictly logical thinking of Alexander von Humboldt. His clear allusion to world-wide connections in the movements of populations is surprising, in spite of the fact that this rediscoverer of America 160 years ago, as is well known, had a great gift of observation. (See *Ensayo politico sobre Nueva España*, 3rd ed., Paris, 1836, chapter VII, p.259 and chapter VI, p.220.)

APPENDIX

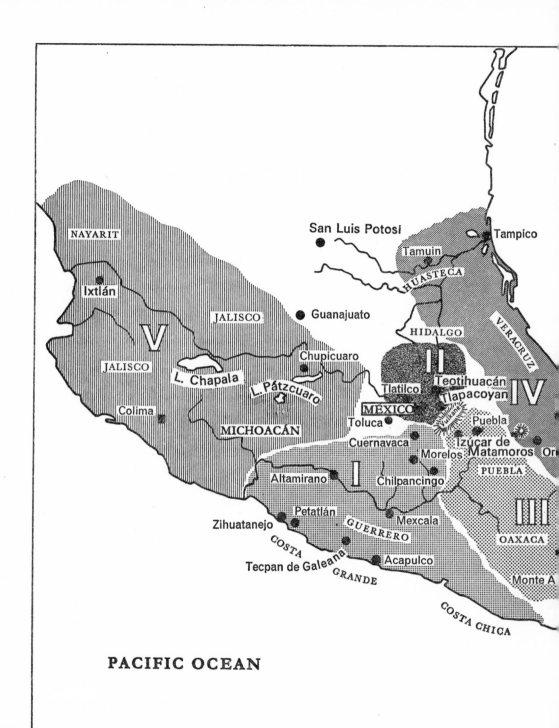

PACIFIC OCEAN

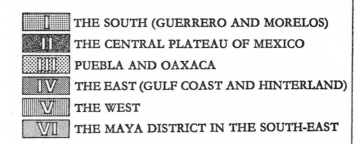

GULF OF MEXICO

Chichén Itzá

Uxmal

Jaina

YUCATÁN

VI

...adas
Veracruz

San Andrés Tuxtla

VERACRUZ

Tres
Zapotes

San Lorenzo

TABASCO

La Venta

Palenque

CHIAPAS

Bonampák

Tical

...aca

Mitla

Tonalá

GUATEMALA

Kaminaljuyú

Copán

HONDURAS

Guatemala

Chimaltenango

EL SALVADOR

191

BIBLIOGRAPHY

Bamm, P.: An den Küsten des Lichts. Munich, 1961.

Biographie Universelle Ancienne et Moderne, Paris: article 'Gregorio García'.

Bernal, I.: Bibliografía de arqueología y etnografía: Mesoamérica y norte de México. In: Instituto Nacional de Antropología e Historia. Mexico City, 1962.

Bernal, I. and Villaret, B.: Arts anciens du Mexique. Architecture et sculpture. Paris, 1962.

Bossert, H. Th.: Altsyrien. Kunst und Handwerk in Zypern, Syrien, Palästina ... Tübingen, 1951.

Bruns, G.: Antike Terrakotten. Berlin, 1946.

Brush, E. S.: 'Figurines of Coastal Guerrero: their Temporal and Cultural Significance'. In: International Congress of Americanists, Mexico City, 1962, Actas y memorias, vol. I, p. 523.

Caso, A.: Relations between the Old and the New World: a Note on Methodology. In: International Congress of Americanists, Mexico City, 1962, Actas y memorias, vol. I, p. 55.*

Clark, Sir K. M.: The Nude: a Study of Ideal. London, 1956; Harmondsworth, 1960.

Colombia, Banco de la República: El Museo de Oro. Bogotá, 1948.

Covarrubias, M.: Indian Art of Mexico and Central America. New York, 1957.

Covarrubias, M.: Mexico South: the Isthmus of Tehuantepec. London–Norwood, Mass., 1947.

Desroches-Noblecort, C.: Tutankhamen. Translated by Claude. New York–London, 1963.

Disselhoff, H.-D.: Geschichte der altamerikanischen Kulturen. Munich, 1953.

Disselhoff, H.-D. and Linné, S.: Ancient America: the Civilizations of the New World. Translated by Ann E. Keep. ART OF THE WORLD. London, 1961.

Drucker, P.: Ceramic Sequences at Tres Zapotes, Veracruz, Mexico. Smithsonian Institute, Washington, D. C., 1943**.

Duran, Fr. D.: Historia de las Indias de Nueva-España y Islas de Tierra Firme. Mexico City, 1867–1880.

Emmerich, A.: Art before Columbus: the Art of Ancient Mexico from the Archaic Villages

---

* In his contribution to the proceedings of the Congress Dr. Alfonso Caso draws a comparison between a putative Merovingian figure from Regensburg and the 'bearded man' from the Balsas River area in Guerrero reproduced on p. 76, as well as with the specimens mentioned on pp. 51 and 52. This is obviously to take the comparative method *ad absurdum.* I have not included this specimen here, since it seems to me that it is of no use in our context. The two pieces are only linked externally, whereas their most important inner features display marked differences. The Regensburg figure is of a thoroughly Germanic personage, whereas the Guerrero terracotta doubtless represents an alien non-Germanic type, and can indeed be interpreted as a representation of the God Bes. In drawing such comparisons only the actual content of the artist's conception, not superficial similarities between two objects, can be of any value.

** Of special interest here are the Negroid figures in plate 51 and the lavish material illustrative of Lirios types, of which an overwhelming number have white features (plates 55 f.) and in the present author's view should be regarded as portraits of real individuals. *p. 66.*

of the 2nd Millennium BC to the Splendour of the Aztecs. New York, 1963.

Feuchtwanger, F. and Groth-Kimball, I.: The Art of Ancient Mexico. London–New York, 1954.

Flores Guerrero, R.: Historia general del arte mexicano. Mexico City, 1962.

García, Fr. G.: Origen de los Indios del Nuevo Mundo, e Indias Occidentales. 1st ed. Valencia, 1607; 2nd ed. Madrid, 1729.

García Granados, R.: 'Antigüedades mexicanas en Europa'. In: Academia Mexicana de la Historia, Memorias, vol. I, 1942.

García Payón, J.: 'Cultura de El Tajín'. In: México Prehispánico. Mexico City, 1946.

Groth-Kimball, I.: Mayan Terracottas. London, 1960–New York, 1960, 1961.

Guzmán, E.: 'Caracteres fundamentales del arte. XI. El arte indigena'. In: México Prehispánico. Mexico City, 1946.

Hofstätter, H. H. and Pixa, H.: Vergleichende Weltgeschichte. Baden-Baden, 1963.

Hornius, G.: De originibus americanis. The Hague, 1652.

Humboldt, F. H. A. von: Political Essay on the Kingdom of New Spain. Translated by J. Black. London, 1811.

Irwin, C. H.: Fair Gods and Stone Faces. New York, 1963.

Jiménez Moreno, W.: 'Síntesis de la historia pretolteca de Mesoamérica'. In: Esplendor del México Antiguo. Mexico City, 1959.

Jiménez Moreno, W.: Historia de México. Mexico City, 1963.

Kelemen, P.: Medieval American Art: Masterpieces of the New World before Columbus. New York, 1966.

Kidder, A. II: 'Rediscovering America'. In: Horizon, vol. 6, 1964, no. 3.

Kidder, A. II and Samayoa Chinchilla, C.: Art of the Ancient Maya. Catalogue. Detroit Institute of Arts. Detroit, 1959.

Kirchhoff, P.: 'El papel de México en la América precolombina'; 'El problema del origen de la civilización Mexicana'; 'México y su influencia en el Continente'. In: México Prehispánica. Mexico City, 1946.

Krickeberg, W.: Altmexikanische Kulturen. Berlin, 1956.

Kutscher, G.: Präkolumbische Kunst aus Mexico und Mittelamerika. Frankfurt-on-Main, 1960.

Lehmann, H.: Pre-Columbian Ceramics. London, 1962.

Lehmann, W.: Altmexikanische Kunstgeschichte. Berlin, 1921.

León, N.: Códice Sierra. Mexico City, 1933.

Lothrop, S. K., Foschag, W. and Mahler, J.: Precolumbian Art: The Robert Woods Bliss Collection. New York, 1957.

Malraux, A.: Voices of Silence. Translated by S. Gilbert. New York, 1953; London, 1954.

Marquina, I.: Arquitectura prehispánica. Mexico City, 1951.

Martínez del Río, P.: 'El polamiento primitivo de América'. In: México Prehispánico. Mexico City, 1946.

Mertz, H.: The Wine Dark Sea: Homer's Heroic Epic of the North Atlantic. Chicago, 1964.

Mode, H.: Indische Frühkulturen und ihre Beziehungen zum Westen. Basle, 1944.

Noriega, R., Cook de Leonard, C., and Moctezuma, J. R.: articles in: Esplendor del México Antiguo. Mexico City, 1959.

Noguera, E.: 'Cultura arcaica' and other contributions in: México Prehispánico. Mexico City, 1946.

Northrop, F. S. C.: The Meeting of East and West. New York, 1947.

Pallottino, M.: The Art of the Etruscans. London–New York, 1955.

Pérez de Barradas, J.: El Museo del Oro. Bogotá, 1948.

Peterson, F. A.: Ancient Mexico: an Introduction to the Prehispanic Cultures. New York, 1959.

Picard, G. and Charles-Picard, C.: La vie quotidienne à Carthage au temps d'Hannibal. Paris, 1958.

Piña Chán, R.: Las culturas preclásicas de la cuenca de México. Mexico City, 1955.

Piña Chán, R.: Tlatilco. Mexico City, 1958.

Piña Chán, R.: Mesoamérica. Mexico City, 1960.

Piña Chán, R. and Covarrubias, L.: El pueblo del jaguar. Mexico City, 1964.

Pijoán y Soteras, J.: Summa Artis. (Historia general del arte, vol. 10.) Madrid, 1946.

Pompa y Pompa, A.: 'Tres ensayos historicos de tema mexicano'. In: Memorias y Revista de la Academia Nacional de Ciencias, Mexico City, 1958.

Proskouriakoff, T.: Varieties of Classic Veracruz Sculpture. Washington, 1954.

Rivet, P.: Les origines de l'homme américain. Paris, 1957.

Ruppert, K., Thompson, J. E. S. and Proskouriakoff, T.: Bonampak, Chiapas, Mexico. Washington, 1955.

Sahagún, Fr. B. de: General History of the Things of New Spain; Florentine Codex. Santa Fe, N. Mex., 1950–9.

Seler, C.: Auf alten Wegen in Mexiko und Guatemala. Stuttgart, 1925.*

Seler, E.: Gesammelte Abhandlungen zur amerikanischen Sprache und Alterthumskunde, vols. 1–5. Berlin, 1902–23.

Spratling, W. P.: More Human than Divine: an Intimate and Lively Self-Portrait in Clay of a Smiling People from Ancient Vera Cruz. Mexico City, 1960.

Stirling, M. W.: 'Culturas de la région olmeca'. In: México Prehispánico. Mexico City, 1946.

Stirling, M. W.: Stone Monuments of Southern Mexico. Washington, 1943.

Thompson, J. E. S.: The Rise and Fall of Maya Civilisation. Norman, Okla., 1954.

Toscano, S.: Arte precolumbino de México y de la América central. Mexico City, 1952.

Toscano, S., Kirchhoff, P. and Rubín de la Borbolla, D. F.: Arte precolumbino de México. Mexico City, 1946.

Trimborn, H.: Das alte Amerika. (Grosse Kulturen der Frühzeit, new series.) Stuttgart, 1959.

Ubbelohde-Doering, H.: The Art of Ancient Peru. New York, 1952.**

* Frau Cecilie Seler deserves credit for having photographed for the first time the petroglyphs of Cozamaluapan, Guatemala, mentioned on p. 129, some of which are now on display in the entrance hall to the Staatliche Museen, Berlin-Dahlem. With astonishing zeal this distinguished lady, the wife of the famous Americanist, Eduard Seler, traced the largest relief in this group, measuring four metres in height, which contains as its central figure one of the most monumental human images in ancient American art. One gains the impression that the artist was here concerned to carve out of the natural stone a veritable heroic figure. The realistic conception and character of the energetic young man who confronts us shows that he is not Semitic but indisputably a white man, and thus of the utmost significance for our evaluation of certain historical events which must have taken place in the New World. According to Krickeberg the petroglyphs belong to the early Classic period.

** The best figure among the exceptionally fine 'human images' of the Mochica culture in Peru, mentioned on p. 161, are to be found in this volume by the well-known German scholar.

Unger, E.: 'Semiten'. In: Reallexikon der Vorgeschichte. Berlin, 1928.

Vaillant, G.: The Aztecs of Mexico. London, 1950.

Vaillant, G.: 'A Bearded Mystery'. In: Natural History, vol. 31, New York, 1931, no. 3.

Vaillant, G.: 'La cerámica'. In: México Prehispánico. Mexico City, 1946.

Vivó Jorge, A.: 'Las razas indígenas', 'Culturas de Guerrero' and other contributions in: México Prehispánico. Mexico City, 1946.

Westheim, P.: Arte antiguo de México. Mexico City, 1950.

Westheim, P.: La cerámica del México antiguo. Mexico City, 1962.

Westheim, P.: La escultura del México antiguo. Mexico City, 1963.

Winter, F.: Die Typen der figürlichen Terrakotten. Berlin, 1903.

---

* The concept of Semites on which the present volume is based rests upon the clear statements made by this writer.

INDEX

The numerals in italics refer to the plates and figures.